LIVE
from
MIDDLE AMERICA

LIVE
from
MIDDLE AMERICA

☆ ☆ ☆

RANTS FROM A
RED-STATE COMEDIAN

Brad Stine

HUDSON
STREET
PRESS

HUDSON STREET PRESS
Published by Penguin Group
Penguin Group (USA) Inc., 375 Hudson Street, New York, New York 10014, USA
Penguin Group (Canada), 90 Eglinton Avenue East, Suite 700, Toronto, Ontario, Canada M4P 2Y3
(a division of Pearson Penguin Canada Inc.)
Penguin Books Ltd., 80 Strand, London WC2R 0RL, England
Penguin Ireland, 25 St. Stephen's Green, Dublin 2, Ireland (a division of Penguin Books Ltd.)
Penguin Group (Australia), 250 Camberwell Road, Camberwell, Victoria 3124, Australia
(a division of Pearson Australia Group Pty. Ltd.)
Penguin Books India Pvt. Ltd., 11 Community Centre, Panchsheel Park, New Delhi – 110 017, India
Penguin Books (NZ), cnr Airborne and Rosedale Roads, Albany, Auckland 1310, New Zealand
(a division of Pearson New Zealand Ltd.)
Penguin Books (South Africa) (Pty.) Ltd., 24 Sturdee Avenue, Rosebank, Johannesburg 2196, South Africa

Penguin Books Ltd., Registered Offices: 80 Strand, London WC2R 0RL, England

First published by Hudson Street Press, a member of Penguin Group (USA) Inc.

First Printing, March 2006
10 9 8 7 6 5 4 3 2 1

REGISTERED TRADEMARK—MARCA REGISTRADA
HUDSON
STREET
PRESS

LIBRARY OF CONGRESS CATALOGING-IN-PUBLICATION DATA

Stine, Brad.
    Live from middle America : rants from a red-state comedian / Brad Stine.
        p. cm.
    ISBN 1-59463-015-1 (hardcover : alk. paper)
    1. Conservatism—United States.   2. Liberalism—United States.   3. United States—Politics
and government—21st century.   4. United States—Religion—21st century.   5. United States—
Social conditions—21st century.   I. Title.
    HN59.2.S744 2006
    973.93102'07—dc22

                                                                                2005028979

Printed in the United States of America
Set in Adobe Garamond

To Wyatt and Maycee . . . yes, you can come in

☆ ACKNOWLEDGMENTS ☆

Special thanks to:

My wife, Desiree, who insists that she told me to write a book ten years ago; and now that I have, I apparently owe her new bedroom furniture.

Laureen Rowland, my faithful publisher/editor, who believed in me and ignored the fact that I believe that paragraphs and punctuation are for the weak.

Mike Smith, my manager, who is in therapy trying to keep me from sticking my foot in my mouth.

Mel Berger, my agent. You have done a great job for me, even though you claim to be a liberal. Fear not as I lead you to the Promised Land.

Adam Green, who wrote an amazing article about me in the *New Yorker*, which got me this deal. A good man who deserves more than just this accolade, but, unfortunately, I'm tapped out, what with the aforementioned manager and agent taking their cuts.

To my late dad, who taught me to be a conservative, and my mom, who taught me to be a Christian.

This has been an amazing ride. . . . I wonder where it will land.

Nothing matters but God.

☆ Contents ☆

Who I Am and Why You Can't Live Without Me

I must admit, when I was first asked to write a book about my thoughts on our great country, I was blown away. I'm a comedian for crying out loud. Only in America would they look to the village idiot for his views on life, politics, and religion.

You may already know who I am, having seen me on the Promise Keepers tour, on TV, or headlining your local comedy club, shocking you with the concept that a comic can make you laugh despite the handicap of not using the "F" word. If you don't know who I am, that can only mean one thing: You are a liberal. Put the book down and back slowly away from the display table. You belong in the self-help section. Turn around. And run.

Only in America would they look to the village idiot for his views on life, politics, and religion.

Now, there are three things you need to know about me right off the bat. First, I am a conservative comedian. That's right, a *conservative* comedian, one of two known to exist in the Western Hemisphere (and the other isn't funny). I am both a fiscal and *social* conservative, which is light-years apart from the more liberal Schwarzeneggeresque conservative who loves fiscal conservative policies but still votes for liberal social issues so he can keep his job with the Hollywood liberal elite, making the big money that fiscal conservatives let him keep. ("C'mon, Arnold, for the Terminator, that's kind of a wussy attitude," I quip, safely hidden behind my laptop, in Tennessee, under an assumed name.)

Second, I am a Christian, which simply means I share the same religious beliefs and/or worldviews as ALL of our Founding Fathers. Yes, you heard me, Barbara Boxer, ALL OF THEM! (I'll talk more about that later, and it won't be pretty.)

Third, I believe the United States of America is the greatest country that has ever existed on the face of the earth. That our country is better than all the other countries combined, and that we've created, defended, and instilled more good toward more nations than any other country, ever.

So, because of these three beliefs, when I die, by act of Congress, I will be stuffed and mounted and sent to the Smithsonian Institution and placed in the "Why he never got his own sitcom" display. But before I go any further, I don't want to give you the impression that this is just another one of those partisan "liberals are always wrong and conservatives are always right" books. No, my hope is that, after reading this book, you'll easily be able to draw that conclusion on your own.

When I die, by act of Congress, I will be stuffed and mounted and sent to the Smithsonian Institution and placed in the "Why he never got his own sitcom" display.

As much as I have made a tidy living in the last few years making fun of the politically correct and the fanatically out-of-touch Left, the truth is, when all is said and done, I actually am interested in seeking some common ground. Even though I have been labeled conservative, I actually consider myself more of a commonsense comedian. I guess that's why the conservative POV resonates more with me: because I see it as a viewpoint that demands, more than anything, allegiance to personal responsibility. (That's the way I was raised, anyway. My dad, God rest his soul, taught me that I could be anything I wanted to be IF I was willing to work hard enough. I was poor growing up, but I was never aware of it. Probably because I was constantly unconscious from hunger. Nevertheless, when I did come to, I wasn't expecting any handouts.)

Now, I realize that no one believes anything that doesn't stem directly from their own bias. Though as a conservative with an open mind—which is more than I can say for every liberal I have ever encountered—I will admit that even conservatives aren't always perfect. We are always RIGHT, but not perfect.

I'm not a political analyst or a Republican pundit or an expert on the elements of governmental processes. (Then again, as I have come to observe, neither are most liberals.) I don't know the names of all the players in the political system. I am just an everyman, with a few strong opinions and a stage from which to rant. And, as it turns out, an audience of hundreds of millions of Middle Americans who happen to subscribe to the same ideals and ideas that I do, chief among them that the conservative view is actually more rational and intelligent than the liberal view.

The fact is, the liberal lives in a world he wants to think exists (though it never will), while the conservative lives in a world that actually *does*. Case in point: The politically correct movement, that hideous stain on American culture that has created widespread destruction, was manufactured and instituted by the liberal. If *anything* should encourage intellectual fence-sitters that the conservative viewpoint is superior to the liberal, it would be the desire to not be associated with a mind-set that believes that offending someone is worse than speaking the truth. As a comedian, I don't have that problem. I offend everybody.

You will notice, as you read this book, that there is a very specific connection between the conservative worldview and the Judeo-Christian ethic. The conservative movement is indebted to this religious belief, whether it acknowledges it or not, for substantively forming its concept as to who humans are and how we should behave. Most liberals, on the other hand, don't take

> The liberal lives in a world he wants to think exists, while the conservative lives in a world that actually *does*.

time to consider how or why they have arrived at the irrational conclusions they have about life, and that is something I hope this book will showcase (hilariously, of course).

I'm sure some liberal critics will read this book and complain that I'm taking enormous liberties by blaming everything that's wrong with Americans on the liberals; that my observations are based on broad, sweeping generalizations and unfair stereotypes. I can only respond to this by saying . . . that's what makes it so much fun!

For too long, the best comics have performed from severely Left-leaning points of view. For those conservatives and/or Christians out there who have been looking to the heavens for a comedian to champion their beliefs, I humbly offer my services.

Wrapped neatly in a package of political correctness, with a touch of tolerance, baked in a cream pie, and shoved into the liberals' faces.

Let the games begin!

—Brad Stine

The South Really Does Exist—and Not Just in the Movies

I was interviewed on Tucker Carlson's excellent PBS television show *just* before the 2004 election, and, after taping, he was kind enough to give me and my manager a lift in his Volvo to the D.C. restaurant where we were heading. (A little heads-up for anyone grabbing a ride with "Tuck" in the future: He not only thinks and dresses like a conservative, but drives like one as well. The ones you find every weekend at a NASCAR event. Not watching mind you, but participating! Clearly, as a conservative in D.C., he's been conditioned to speak his mind and then escape before the posse can be rounded up.)

Anyway, as we drove along, I asked him (raising my voice above the screams of mortally wounded pedestrians), "Who do you think is going to win the election?"

"I don't think it's going to be Bush," he replied, "because of Iraq."

"Bush will win," I told him confidently. "You've just been hanging around too many liberals. You need to get out of this town and come to the red states for a while." (You hang with liberals, you begin to think like them. Then again, you hang with psychotics, you begin to think like THEM, too—though I realize I'm being redundant.)

Well, Tucker, I told you we were going to kick butt! You owe me a bow tie!

> You hang with liberals, you begin to think like them. Then again, you hang with psychotics, you begin to think like THEM, too—though I realize I'm being redundant.

The reason I felt so confident about Bush's reelection is because I now live in Nashville, Tennessee. For those of you reading this book who reside in either Los Angeles or New York City, Nashville is a small town nestled in the middle of the picturesque state of Tennessee. A state, you may be stunned to discover, that is actually part of your country. I have to qualify that because, from what I have discovered while interacting with persons from the fringe coasts, they believe Middle America is actually a make-believe world that was created by Walt Disney to give the illusion that at one time in our nation's history, moms baked pies as opposed to microwaving them.

There is no more blatant fact that I have observed performing in both of these metropolitan cities than the following: Those who inhabit them AND make the decisions as to how America will be portrayed on TV have never, EVER, been to Middle America. In fact, the only time they may have even glimpsed it was out the plane window while flying over it, nestled in first class, all the while harping on why the merlot doesn't finish with less tannin.

Nevertheless, Middle America makes up, by far, most of who America is and how we think (a thought process, I might add, that is virtually impossible for the liberals to wrap their minds around). Now I *thought* I knew what living in a conservative community felt like because I lived in Orange County, California, for years. Anyone who believes all conservatives are exactly the same, try living in Southern California for thirty years and then move to Nashville. California's a blue state, Tennessee's red. Liberals who consider themselves free thinkers spend every waking moment censoring their thoughts and everyone else's all the while thinking they're making the world a better place. The honesty and freedom red-state civilians enjoy by not trapping themselves in some self-imposed liberal paranoia of possibly offending someone is a beauty to behold.

You want proof that there are millions of Americans who are completely unaffected by the politically correct spin that dominates the media? Move to the South—not Florida. Not Atlanta, Georgia. The *real* South. I mean, the South GROWS tobacco for crying out loud! It's a cash crop for these people, and they don't think twice about the implications of manufacturing cigarettes,

In California, it's illegal to smoke pretty much anywhere within the borders of the state, whereas in Tennessee, it's illegal NOT to smoke. The state motto of Tennessee? "Chemo's for cowards."

and I say God bless them for that. Packing up my family and moving to Tennessee was a breath of fresh air for me and mine—figuratively, but definitely not literally.

You can't do anything in California anymore without running it past the PC police. For example, in California, it's illegal to smoke pretty much anywhere within the borders of the state, whereas in Tennessee, it's illegal NOT to smoke. Everybody smokes down South.

It would be rough growing up as a child down there because dads are like, "Johnny, you don't get up from that table until you finish your cigarette."

"But, Daddy," Johnny whines, "I don't like menthol."

"You just hush up and finish it, look at your sister eating her Skoal and not saying a word!"

I see grandmothers in wheelchairs toting their own oxygen while SMOKING. Meanwhile, they're babysitting their three-year-old grandchild who is riding her tricycle while SMOKING. You want to find a remnant of rugged individualism in America? Trust me, it's down here! The state motto of Tennessee is "Chemo's for cowards."

There is no question that moving from the big city to Middle America takes some adjustment. Southerners live in the country! They actually have real fields where they grow real crops. They don't have potting soil so they can grow herbs on the balcony of their townhouse, they have something called *dirt*. You see it everywhere, just lying on the ground, and it comes for free in the form of a farm or even a backyard, versus eighty dollars for a ten-pound bag. This was a revelation to a family who had always looked forward to the fall in Southern California so we could take the kids to visit our very own California version of a "country" pumpkin patch. In L.A., that means some straw hay bales strewn around the parking lot at the local mall where kids can come from all around and actually "pick" their own pumpkins—which means "picking" them up off the pavement where they have been neatly stacked right next to the vintage tractor that was hauled in to give the kids that pioneer feeling. This "parking-lot farm" concept takes on a whole new surreal dimension when you move to the actual country. The pumpkin patch in Tennessee is actually a patch of farmland where pumpkins are—now get this—GROWN!

Farmers in Tennessee are not actors pretending to be farmers. In Tennessee, farmers *actually farm*. As much as Hollywood wants to embrace and re-create the rural America it sees in movies, that rural America comes with the knowledge that when you're through embracing it, your nails are never dirty and there will be plenty of time to catch dinner at the Cheesecake Factory where you eat food that real farmers actually grow and harvest. Hmmm. That seems fair.

Another reason I instantly embraced the South was its unabashed pride in tradition. These people hunt and fish, and they don't apologize for it. I love that! There's none of this PC nonsense like "Don't shoot the animals; it might hurt their feelings!" This is the SOUTH, baby; they don't even *pretend* that animals have rights! No, these people see a bunny and they say, "Shoot it, eat it, and make a hat out of the rest." Every animal is seen as a potential accessory. "Is that a snake?" "No, that's a boot right there." Eat it, and if you have a head left over, don't hide it somewhere surreptitiously . . . HANG IT ON YOUR WALL!

There are even roadkill laws down here that state if you kill an animal with your car, you can keep it. The fact that Southerners

This is the SOUTH; they don't even *pretend* that animals have rights! These people see a bunny and they say, "Shoot it, eat it, and make a hat out of the rest."

would want an animal they just ran down with their vehicle is all I need to hear when choosing the kind of people I want on my side when the apocalypse comes. They keep knives and tanning tools in their trunks just in case they're fortunate enough to bag a deer with their pick-up! This is not only testimony to their ingenuity, but humbling to a guy like me who still gets queasy when a waiter brings me a lobster with its head attached.

In the South, I realized I had found my own kind. How can you not love a place where liberals are not only the minority, they also make a great throw rug?

After thirty years in blue-state California, I was finally home.

☆ 2 ☆

Nashville, USA

Nashville is one of the coolest cities in the United States. If the red states ever needed a capital, we've found it. Nashville has all the top record labels, top talent agencies, and major stars whose names are Garth, Merle, and Reba—names that don't conform to Hollywood standards but, fortunately, can be easily pronounced, even after being hit in the head with a barstool. Nashville's most famous place to view a raucous kick-butt band is Ryman Auditorium, which, by the way, used to be a church. That's a red state for you. We'll get you to church one way or another.

In many ways, Nashville is like California without the smelly haze that burns your eyes and ruins the view at times (what's that called? oh yeah . . . pretentiousness). Nashville is a conservative version of California, a Conservatifornia, if you will. My dad moved our family to California when I was nine years old, well before anyone realized it was a cult. Only after years of traveling back through red states as a stand-up comedian was I able to recollect, through a brainwashed haze, my formative red-state

Indiana upbringing, where lying, cheating, and self-absorption weren't considered positive attributes, and neighbors were considered friends, not plaintiffs.

Only after years of traveling through red states was I able to recollect my formative red-state upbringing, where lying, cheating, and self-absorption weren't considered positive attributes.

So when I moved my family to Nashville in 2002, I had some pretty major adjustments to make, like having to relearn how to drive. Now, I learned to drive in Southern California. People think that's hard driving? It's EASY, 8 million miles of freeway and just one sign: MAXIMUM SPEED 65 . . . GOOD LUCK . . . GO! See, that's all one should ever have to worry about while driving—how fast you can go. In California, that was the only sign we really needed.

Not in Middle America! There are *way* too many signs on the freeway, and they're never helpful. They're always warning you about something that any blue-stater would assume is a typo. I'm not talking about your basic SLOW DOWN FOR CONSTRUCTION signs that pop up periodically, I'm talking about bizarre signs warning drivers of things I didn't know still existed in the twenty-first century, like warnings for animals that just might *leap out* in front of an oncoming vehicle!

The first time I saw a deer-crossing sign, I yelled, "If they're such a hazard, why do you let them on the road!" If you got deer crossing the freeway, that's not a "put up a sign" problem, that's a "put up a wall" problem! Dig a moat; put them on a leash; something! You know they invented barbed wire 150 years ago? Use it!

Middle Americans are so used to deer jumping out onto the road in front of their cars, they go about their business like that's normal. Yeah, it's normal . . . if you live in a cartoon! But my red-state people see automobiles not just as vehicles, but as weapons, sometimes as effective as a Smith & Wesson. Whatever it takes to put meat on the table. Where else can a Sunday drive with the kids potentially result in a month's supply of venison and jerky? In the South, every day's a good day to hunt. That's why liberals are against hunting. Driven by emotion, liberals see even Lyme disease–spreading deer as Bambi . . . conservatives just see deer as *Bam!*

In the South, every day's a good day to hunt. Liberals see even Lyme disease–spreading deer as Bambi . . . conservatives just see them as Bam!

Lest you think that a deer-crossing sign is an aberration, consider the signs that are written in cryptic, shorthand code, stuff like BRIDGE ICES BEFORE ROAD. Huh? I'm like, "OK . . . noted . . . so . . . what do I actually do with this information!?" People are passing me, meanwhile I'm trying to wrestle my snowshoes on while driving and I'm screaming "Help me! . . . The bridge is going to do . . . something! . . . Watch out for deer!!"

I think the sign that reminds me most that I no longer live in the land of palm trees is the one that reads WATCH OUT FOR TRACTORS. Tractors? On the highway? Now, I'm no farmer mind you, but don't they have some kind of designated, oh I don't know . . . FIELD they're supposed to be in? Is that what happens in the South, farmers just run wild periodically? Calling out to their fellow farmers, "Hey Clem, grab a combine, let's hit the freeway! Whew, slow 'er down, boy, I got this baby up to . . . three! Let's go race the Amish!" (That's right, folks, when all else fails, make fun of the Amish. Why? Because they have no electronic recording equipment to prove I said anything! And even if they got their hands on some, they would have nowhere to plug it in.)

Sometimes, signs are placed on the highway to prepare you for the unimaginable, from alligators to armadillos, either of which if spotted on the road in a blue state would be cause to confiscate that part of the freeway and designate it as a wetland. Other times, they are placed to remind you just how lazy some Americans have become, thanks to the liberal idea that maintains that hard work is no longer noble or necessary. Remember, folks, for many years, Democrats controlled the South, years that happened to coincide with the emergence of interstate travel, so I'll let you draw your own conclusions. Driving through my new community recently, I actually happened upon a sign that said BUMP. That's all it said, BUMP. It didn't even have punctuation, so it was a kind of quiet, matter-of-fact sign. And, just in case I missed the point, there was an arrow pointing toward the pavement showing me exactly where the bump would be.

For many years, Democrats controlled the South, years that happened to coincide with the emergence of interstate travel. I'll let you draw your own conclusions.

Trust me, folks—I don't claim to be an expert when it comes to the best use of county funds for road repair and infrastructure refurbishing. But I'm thinking, if you have enough money to craft a bump sign and you have enough excess cash to hire people to go out and install the bump sign, here's something you may want to consider . . . fix the bump.

Maybe it's time to take some money out of the bump-sign slush fund and reallocate it to the bump-repair pork-barrel legislation your congressman is trying to ram through Congress? I don't know, call me crazy, but to me, this makes sense! The dang bump signs don't even work, because by the time you see them, doing 75 m.p.h., you only have enough time to consider why your transmission is lying in the middle of the fast lane.

I believe signs should exist to prepare you to avoid a possible catastrophe, not just to inform you what's about to happen whether you like it or not. I don't know about you, but I don't want to be traveling seventy down the freeway only to encounter a sign reading GIANT HOLE. Whoops, too late. Would it have killed you to warn me about the hole prior to my arrival in it? I don't want the oh-so-informative road sign to become the lazy man's way to avoid responsibility. And yet, that is the precedent the pre–red state Southern liberals have established. As long as we inform you in writing about every possible nuance of danger potentially inherent in the scenario you are about to embark upon, we are free and clear from any responsibility that should have been yours in the first place! Don't forget, the liberal always believes it's the other person's responsibility to be one step ahead of your incompetence.

Yes, living in Nashville was going to be a wonderful experience for me and mine. Sure, there were some things that we'd need to get used to, but if that's what it took to purge any leftover liberal influence from my mortal soul in order to ensure my salvation, it would be well worth it.

Now if you'll excuse me, I gotta run. The kids are out of cigarettes.

In the Beginning, There Was No Whining

The first Europeans arrived here by boat. We're not talking *QE2,* here. Back then, boat travel was hard. Boats were small, cramped, and didn't have room for a shuffleboard game or an all-you-can-eat buffet.

What is so incredible about this first wave of would-be Americans is how hearty they had to be to endure such a trip. It took months and months of travel over rough seas and through stormy weather, and still they came. There was sickness and death, and still they came. Such was the motivation behind a people who were driven to a land that would offer them freedom to worship their God unimpeded, but also brought the added bonus of being even farther away from France. And, most amazingly, not only were they willing to endure this difficult voyage no matter the unpleasantness that lay ahead, they even brought their kids!

These brave souls brought their sons and daughters on a six-month boat journey, and the kids didn't complain. (They threw

These people were driven to a land that would offer them freedom to worship their God unimpeded, with the added bonus of being even farther away from France.

up a lot, but they didn't complain.) Why? Because, back then, parents disciplined their children without threat of legal ramifications. That's right, just in case my point is not completely clear, let me spell it out: Back then, you could actually S-P-A-N-K your kid's hind end. Notice I didn't say "beat," "hit," "attack," "flog," "punch," or even "pummel." There was a time when a spank or swat on the butt—used sparingly—was a very effective technique for teaching kids that there are consequences to their actions. Only someone who has never had kids would consider spanking inappropriate (i.e., liberal policymakers).

I'm sure somebody out there reading this is saying, "Hey, liberals have kids, too!" But calling a liberal's kid their "kid" could lead one to mistakenly assume that the liberal parent actually has some control over his or her offspring. God knows liberals have fought hard to ensure that their kids enjoy as little parental authority as possible. Kids aren't kids to liberals;

Kids aren't kids to liberals; they're business partners, associates, and/or roommates who need braces.

they're business partners, associates, and/or roommates who need braces.

And for those out there who subscribe to the "spanking teaches kids to hit" theory, trust me—any kid who needs a spanking is already quite proficient at hitting. In fact, sometimes that's *what they're being spanked for.* Funny, we never hear liberals making the argument that putting someone in jail is teaching them how to hold others against their will. But expecting to find consistency and logic in liberal arguments is apparently asking too much.

Discipline is crucial to establishing boundaries for kids who desperately need to know they are loved enough to be told no. That's what corporal punishment can do for a culture: create kids who welcome a six-month boat journey, complete with salted meats and scurvy, and who then appreciate setting foot on solid ground simply because the trip was so bad.

So the early Americans arrived and settled the whole Eastern seaboard, but soon that wasn't enough. Everyone was shocked to discover just how large this great land was. So began the American spirit of discovery and adventure that has informed and inspired every American legacy and tradition since. That, and the hope of selling someone something. Go West, young capitalist.

It's for certain, the early pioneers weren't liberals. Sure, they were rebels, but they didn't expect anything to be handed to them without earning it. They didn't know exactly what they were getting into, but whatever it was, it was their decision to try, and no matter the outcome, they had no one to blame or praise but themselves. Had the first pioneers been liberals, they would have most certainly left their kids in day care, thus allowing their pioneer women the joy of feeling empowered while wearing petticoats in hundred-degree heat.

Had the first pioneers been liberals, they would have most certainly left their kids in day care.

These families traveled for months, through snowstorms and deserts, attacks from Indians, and threats from wild animals, and still the kids didn't complain. They didn't have Game Boys, or DVDs, or MP3 players. Yet still, somehow, the covered-wagon kids figured out ways to pass the time without batteries. The kids weren't constantly harping, "Are we there yet?" because there was no "there" yet.

There were no McDonald's Happy Meals, either. Imagine that, back then, kids thought *food itself* was prize enough, even if the meal didn't include a toy! (No wonder kids think society owes them something when we act like eating warrants compensation. In third-world countries, kids receive a reward for eating, too . . . they don't starve.)

Finally, after years (no one knows how many, as day planners hadn't been invented yet), the early Americans settled the West, thus resulting in the humble beginnings of the greatest country there ever was. It was decided that the people would rule the land, not kings. Freedom, the chance to reach your highest potential based solely on your own efforts, without handouts, became "the American way." For what we consider the American spirit was, in reality, the human spirit finally unshackled from caste systems, monarchies, and the privileged few whose only accomplishment was being born into the right family or, in the case of models, with the right bone structure.

More people want into this country than any other country in the world. Why is that? Because of our intolerance for other cultures? No, exactly the opposite. It's because you can experience *your own culture* right here in America, freely and without the limitations that are inherent in nondemocratic societies, such as forced labor camps for people who believe in God, or theocratic or atheistic countries that refuse to allow women to attend school but make up for it by imposing female circumcision and forced abortions. As we have seen in recent years, if your desire to accomplish something is so passionate that you're willing to die for it, there's pretty much nothing anyone can do to stop you.

It was that kind of attitude that created this country. If you look around, you'll see that even people who threaten to leave us, when push comes to shove, never actually do. Like Barbra Streisand and Alec Baldwin. They both threatened to leave if Bush W. was elected the first time. They're still here. Baldwin's been rumored to be eyeing a career in politics, and a fine politician he would be. His brother, who became a Christian a couple years ago, says that Alec told him the reason he didn't leave was because President Bush wasn't elected, he was *selected*. How Clintonesque. There is definitely a bright future in politics for a guy who has already mastered the art of waffling, hedging, and reinterpreting results to rationalize his actions and further his own desires. And Barbra's presence gives all Americans the hope that we'll finally get to see the long-awaited sequel *Yentl 2,* in which she's back, and this time she WANTS to marry the chick!

The one thing illegal aliens have grasped that the majority of the citizens of this great country seem to have lost sight of is that it's hard to get here, and it's WORTH the struggle. The

America that had to fight and scrape for every freedom it acquired is still the Holy Grail for many millions of immigrants who arrive on our shores daily, though landing on the "shores" of the Rio Grande without a boat and then not letting the rest of us in on the fact that you're here is a dilemma that must be rectified. Of course, the liberal won't call aliens "illegal," only "undocumented," which is the first time in American history that liberals haven't required bureaucratic paperwork. Not condemning illegal immigration with the hope that one day these people will vote Democrat is apparently what liberals meant when they said they needed a moral value to champion.

The liberal unwillingness to hold anyone to any kind of standard is precisely why, in this age of terror, we can't afford to have liberals running the country. Of course, had liberals been spanked now and again growing up, we wouldn't have these problems.

I told you so.

☆ 4 ☆

Who Ya Callin' Stupid?

America is home to 59 million stupid people. Yessiree, you read it here. As the postelection shock of '04 put tens of thousands more of America's liberals into therapy, they were able to survive only by taking their counselors' advice and building their own effigies of George W. Bush. Problem was, they're liberals, which makes an effigy less practical. They can't burn it, since it would pollute the environment, and they can't beat it, since that would promote violence. So most of them ended up selling them on eBay and donating the proceeds to a "protect the belching termite" fund or any number of like causes that put bugs on par with humans, which liberals seem to love.

It was great sport to watch the (liberal) political pundits and newspeople continue to try and find the missing link that once again brought their belief system to its knees. There was, of course, the old scapegoat that they simply didn't "get their message out" until one of the higher-ranking Democratic strategists came up with the novel notion of actually finding a message first before trying to sell it. Because the exit polls introduced the idea that Americans were (suddenly!) concerned about morals, liberals saw this as a clue toward their next offensive: Let's find a moral of our own!

Because the exit polls introduced the idea that Americans were concerned about morals, liberals said, "Let's find a moral of our own!"

Poverty was the first issue that came to mind. Poverty is perfect for liberals because most Democrats are rich; this is therefore a cause they can champion while eating buffalo mozzarella with olive tapenade and sun-dried tomatoes (on ciabatta) in the backs of their limos. In fact, poverty is the only moral issue, post–'04 election, I have ever heard liberals speak of that's been mentioned in the Bible. If the 2004 election taught Democrats anything, it's that in order to have a chance at winning over moral America, they'd better learn how to fake a moral conviction. It should seem apparent that if your party has to search for a moral value, you've got some problems. This, from the group that has abandoned any notion of decency as being too "intrusive."

So, clearly, it's my responsibility as a conservative Christian American—and yours, too—to teach our fellow Americans a thing or two about who we are, and why they will never win another election if they don't "figure us out," and fast. First, they may want to consider the fact that conservative Americans are a little, how should I say, "put out" by the fact the liberal-minded elite constantly refers to us as stupid. Just for starters, that may not be the best way to bring people into your camp. I've heard it all on this point, from a London paper asking how 59 million Americans could be so dumb as to elect this president, to a well-known liberal personality referring to us as trailer trash on *The O'Reilly Factor*.

Now that I live in the South it's much more apparent to me how blatantly malicious the liberal mind is toward the alleged mental competence of people who live in this region. The reason liberals stereotype Southerners in this way is no doubt because of their accent, something they of course have no control over. Anytime Hollywood wants to represent a real dufus in movies or on TV, the lazy writer's solution is to give them a Southern accent. How about *Hee Haw, Green Acres,* and the *Beverly Hillbillies*? Why do you think we never see any Nobel Prize–winning scientists coming from the South, regardless of the fact that some of the best universities in the country are here? It's because of the Southern accent. The molecular biologist or quantum physicist never comes from the South because no matter what they invented, the liberals wouldn't want it. Picture a scientist in his laboratory in the deep South yelling, "Whoooeee! I reckon I just figerd out a cure fer cancer, whooo!" What would the liberals say?

Why do you think we never see any Nobel Prize-winning scientists from the South? Picture a scientist in his laboratory yelling, "Whoooeee! I reckon I just figerd out a cure fer cancer, whooo!" What would the liberals say? "Uh, that's cool Jethro, you have fun with that, we'll stick with chemo!"

"Uh, that's cool Jethro, you have fun with that, we'll stick with chemo, but thanks for trying!"

It's a form of bigotry, from those who would profess never to be bigots, that is not only unwarranted but is downright disrespectful. Not to mention the fact that we, the so-called stupid contingent, won the dang election. So, let's see, if logic prevails (and I know it doesn't for the liberal), it would seem to me that the winners (that would be us) are smart and the LOSERS (that would be the liberals) are stupid.

What better evidence do we need of this than the fact that at the hands of liberals there are way more lawsuits and far fewer aerosol cans? They demand that products be manufactured to make it impossible for idiots (like them) to hurt themselves. Every time you make a product that's too safe, you are sucking the backbone out of your citizens. I am not anti-safety, I just remember a time when, because some products were potentially dangerous, you actually had to be smart enough to be careful.

If we are going to survive as a nation, maybe we need to make it dangerous to drive again. That's why I propose we go back to cars without air bags. That's right, no air bags. Think about the fact that kids who are under the age of twenty have never been in a bagless car. When I was growing up, cars actually had dashboards made out of METAL! None of this namby-pamby Euro plastic car dash crap. You got in a wreck? . . . You paid for it. If you survived, you and your newly constructed jaw went back out on the road a little wiser and a lot more careful. If you didn't make it, you were weeded out so the good drivers had more room to speed on the freeway.

Every car kids ride in nowadays has air bags in every possible location. We've got a front bag, a side bag, a bag for your passenger, a bag for your cell phone. Bags, bags, bags. Kids today probably think the Model T had an air bag. (Well, it might have, but it wasn't a sophisticated gadget, just a midget inflating a paper sack.) And who can blame them; our kids are weak! They've spent their lives in cars with air bags, sitting in the passenger seat wearing a MANDATORY seat belt. I used to sit in the front seat, no seat belt, no air bag, and you know what saved me in a head-on collision? Mom's arm. That's how rugged little kids were expected to fend for themselves back then. If Mom got into a wreck and couldn't whip that arm out fast enough to decapitate us, she'd just meet us at the emergency room (after dropping off the groceries at home before the ice cream melted).

> If Mom got into a wreck and couldn't whip that arm out fast enough, she'd just meet us at the emergency room (after dropping off the groceries at home before the ice cream melted).

So, there they sit, in a bag-filled car, wearing a mandatory seat belt, strapped tightly into a five-point-harness car seat like they're preparing for a lunar mission. And if that's not enough, they learn how to ride a bike wearing a helmet, the big babies! If I had worn a helmet learning to ride my bike, my friends would have beaten me up . . . and they should have! We have gone from a country whose legacy to the world was a functional, free democracy, whose American dream was "You can be anything you want to be if you're willing to work hard enough at it," to a country of morons who need a sign warning them that their coffee is hot.

Maybe helmets for kids are a good idea. However, it's not a good idea to create a delusional world in which kids are taught that pain isn't a part of growing up but an aberration to be avoided at all costs—and when something painful happens to you, as it inevitably will, it's never your fault, but there's always someone to blame.

Preferably someone with assets.

Why Dangerous Toys Are Good for America's Kids

In Indiana, where I lived until I was nine, I went to school with Amish kids who did their schoolwork, went home, and, for fun, built cabinets from hand and churned milk into cheese. They never had, nor do they have, any need for special gadgetry.

In contrast, liberals are masters at creating jobs for themselves by inventing things no one ever needed. Take the liberal atheist scientist. He starts by winning a $15 million government grant to study the effects of livestock flatulence on the atmosphere. When that money runs out and he publishes his results, he'll go out and get a few million more to prove his conclusion was inconclusive and needs further study.

I recently read about a scientist in Wisconsin who developed a laser designed specifically to cut cheese. Funny, I thought we had already figured that out by using that old, archaic, what do you call that gadget? Oh yeah, a knife.

Let's consider the high-tech cheese cutter, shall we? I'm a conservative. I'm all for technology, even if it sometimes comes at the expense of inconveniencing elk, but not the liberal brand of lazy-making inventions that would make even Ron Popeil cry out, "You don't need it!" Imagine the shopper of the future: "Yeah, I need some dish towels, some place settings, and why don't you throw in that particle accelerator!" Any device that requires safety goggles in order to slice food seriously needs to be reconsidered as excessive.

> I'm all for technology, even if it sometimes comes at the expense of inconveniencing elk.

But at the same time that the liberals are wielding a Williams-Sonoma blowtorch in the kitchen so they can concoct the perfect crème brûlée, they're depriving America's children of the sheer fun of a dangerous toy. When I was growing up, there were only a very few situations that could be lethal to a child. One was running with a sucker in your mouth (if you fell, you could choke, or so my mother said). As a kid, I ran a lot, I fell a lot, and I ate a lot of suckers, and I'm still here with my larynx intact. Another pertained to dangerous toys. You remember the phrase, "You'll put somebody's eye out with that." Pretty much every toy that existed in the sixties and early seventies, from Click-Clacks to water-propelled rockets, could put your eye out. Part of the fun of having a toy was the possibility that it *could* hurt you, and I think our parents knew that. It's like fireworks nowadays. Today, you can't even buy a decent sparkler. If you have a firework that has no chance of putting your eye out, it doesn't deserve to be called a firework. Just light a couple matches and call it a night.

As a kid, I ran a lot, I fell a lot, and I ate a lot of suckers, and I'm still here with my larynx intact.

When I was growing up I had a creepy-crawler set, which consisted of an open hot plate that you placed a metal plate upon, onto which you poured some goo. This became superheated until it bubbled like napalm. Afterward, you inserted a metal handle in a slot, removed it, and placed it in water till it boiled over. Then you were left with a rubbery spider in a delicious color that sort of resembled candy that you could swallow and choke on.

THAT was a toy! But, no more. Liberals have replaced the creepy-crawler set where you *made* fake bugs with PBS specials *about* bugs and why they need to be respected and never subjugated, disturbed, or used in scientific experiments that may in some way help humans. After all, that's what embryonic stem cells are for. Leave the critters alone, we'll respect nature by killing our own, thank you very much.

The liberal anti-cool toy lobby believes that, rather than teach children personal responsibility, it is much more crucial to weaken them by creating a "safe environment" in which everybody wins, no one gets hurt, and no one makes bad choices. Much of the fun growing up has been taken away from our kids, all for the sake of safety, be it physical or psychological. Toys used to be designed to stimulate and socialize kids, preparing them for situations that life might bring their way, like confrontations with explosions and pointed objects.

Kids today have grown up with video games and computers. They have DVDs and satellite radio and cell phones and MP3 players, and their parents say, "We had none of this, and they have the audacity to say they're bored!" You know what, it's because they ARE BORED. They are bored by unstimulating games that only engage one of their senses and do much of the thinking for them. They are bored because the only sunshine and exercise and fresh air they're getting is replicated on a television or computer screen. They're not playing cops and robbers, or cowboys and Indians, which, by the way, has taken on the liberal revision of that ever-popular kid game oppressor vs. oppressed. They're not playing house, or store, or doctor, or school. These are the games that were born of our imagination; the situations that familiarized us with everyday life and helped us learn how to interact like normal people. (That's before "normal" became a slur, of course.) Sure, we had video games, but they were located in arcades that our parents had to drive us to, and this didn't happen that often. When it did, you paid twenty-five cents a play, and it cost weeks of allowance to learn to master the game . . . and we appreciated it. Then we went back home and played outside some more.

I miss dangerous games, especially the granddaddy of dangerous family games . . . lawn darts. Anyone living in America under the age of twenty today wouldn't believe that we once lived in a country where the whole family played a game involving twelve-inch darts that weighed seven pounds each and were tossed underhand to land point down in a designated circle on the lawn! This was a game where if you weren't paying attention, you didn't just lose points, you lost your cerebral cortex! This was a toy the whole family could enjoy!

I miss dangerous games, especially lawn darts.

In my opinion, the seventies were the beginning of the end of actually having fun as a child. We were making that transition from "buyer beware" to "buyer retain legal representation." Today, every game and sport runs the risk of being rewritten in the likeness of the liberal wuss. A football play will no longer end with a tackle but with the defense reasoning with the runner to give himself up. The winner of Monopoly will be the guy who shames the owner of Boardwalk to give it away as a spawning ground for organic salmon. And in a final coup d'état, liberals will finally succeed in banishing all games that include any part small enough to fit into a toddler's mouth.

Which pretty much leaves us with a basketball. Good thing they make hundred-dollar sandals that guarantee that white men *can* jump.

☆ **6** ☆

Signals, Signs, and Laws
According to the Liberal

All right, let's talk about common courtesy. What was it, where did it go, and why is it the liberals' fault?

Traditionally, Americans were very conservative. Early Americans knew they had to work together as a team or we would collapse as a nation. Back a hundred or so years ago, in the pioneer days, everybody lived by the term "e pluribus unum" ("out of many, one"), meaning, we actually looked out for each other with a common respect and concern for our neighbors' well-being. Men would tip their hats when females walked by, out of respect for the "weaker" sex. (This reference to women being "weaker" in the Wild West when all that was expected of their daily chores was to skin and cook the meal, hand-wash the clothes, take care of the babies [pre-Pampers], boil water for baths out of kindling they had collected and chopped, and sew torn clothes that they had handmade in the first place makes one wonder what a female corporate executive today could possibly find to complain about.)

Women in the Wild West were expected to skin and cook the meal, boil water for baths out of kindling they'd collected and chopped, sew torn clothes they had handmade in the first place, and take care of babies (pre-Pampers).

It was proper and expected to acknowledge a neighbor (or stranger, for that matter) when we crossed paths because one never knew when one was going to have to call on someone to help defend our homestead or raise a barn. These days, at a time when one could argue it's even more important to have friends and allies who could help defend and support our homestead, we find ourselves isolated, living among strangers. One used to pass a stranger on the street or in the hall, look them straight in the eye, and say "Good morning," or, at least here in the South, the even more personal "Howdy." That evolved into the head nod, which is the least invasive way to acknowledge a fellow being without too much effort or personal interaction. The head nod gave way to the averted-eye strategy, which is as prevalent on the street as it is in an elevator or on public transportation, where you get into the elevator, say nothing to the other occupants, and avoid eye contact by watching the floor numbers tick by.

If you think that the averted-eye strategy sounds rude, it went even further downhill from there to the "What are YOU looking at!" scowl that puts a decidedly De Niro–esque spin on a typically predatory stance in the animal kingdom.

In just a few short generations, we have descended from assuming "the stranger is a potential friend" to "the stranger may be armed." Of course, everyone knows this behavior is rude, but being rude is a behavioral choice that the liberals have demanded be respected, not judged.

In just a few short generations, we have descended from assuming "the stranger is a potential friend" to "the stranger may be armed."

The most obvious forum in which this rudeness plays itself out is on the freeway, the shared space designed to get everyone where they need to go. Of course, sharing is a concept learned in kindergarten, and in the many years since then, most liberals have forgotten its true meaning and replaced it instead with behavior otherwise known as "every liberal for himself." So, in freeway parlance, this means that the lane a liberal is occupying is thought of by him as "his" lane. His desire is to take care of "his" business by getting to "his" destination with the absolute minimum amount of inconvenience and distraction from all the "jerks" (meaning conservatives like me) out there driving in front of him. ("Jerk," in the liberal vocabulary, is a stock term given to anyone who hasn't made it their priority not to inconvenience the liberal.)

Remember turn signals? I wish someone out there would please tell me how we, as a nation, came to decide that using a turn signal has become too much to expect when someone is turning! (I can understand not using it when changing lanes, especially when you're on the cell phone. Using a turn signal can be *so* distracting in a conversation.) But as a conservative, I always signal, since I actually believe in obeying the law, not pondering how it's oppressing us.

I can understand how using a turn signal can be *so* distracting during a cell phone conversation.

Turn signals used to be used because we are all burdened at birth with that unfortunate human design flaw known as "I can't READ YOUR MIND!" It used to be that you'd use your turn signal to let the person behind you know that you were about to merge into the lane they now inhabited and you wanted to COURTEOUSLY let them in on your plan so as to best be able to work together in a coordinated effort to allow each of you to get where you needed to go without crashing into the other. Of course, the liberal-minded narcissist of today turned that concept on its ear by viewing the turn signal of the guy in front of him as a warning *to speed up,* lest he lose face and his hard-earned space (which is subsidized by infrastructure tax allotments).

The liberal approach to other traffic signs is no different and no better. For example, "stop" no longer means stop, it means *roll.* "No parking" doesn't actually mean no parking for *me,* the liberal who is just dropping his wife off to run in but is going to stay in the car (just in case a cop comes) or the liberal who himself just has a quick errand to do and will park in the no-parking zone for just a minute while he runs in to grab whatever it is he needs so desperately that he can't park in a real spot and walk to the store. Common sense would tell you that if you're parked in a no-parking space, even if your hazards are on or you've left your dog in the car as proof that you're coming back *really quickly*; if you're not moving, YOU'RE STILL PARKED! "Merge" means speed up, of course, whereas "yield" means back off, or I'll drive you into the ditch. Sixty-five m.p.h. means eighty, and the fast lane means that the speed limit is negotiable. A yellow light used to mean slow down, the light's going to turn red. NOW it means SPEED UP, the light's about to turn red!

And it's not just traffic signs. "Homemade" means made in a factory, and "made by hand" means somebody's hand pushed the "on" button to a machine. "Freshly baked" means it arrived frozen and we'll heat it up for you. "Keep out of reach of children" means leave this wherever you want, and if your kids get ahold of it . . . sue. More than anything, the liberal has created the expectation that rules are never actually enforceable, but simply suggestions that can be fudged as long as you mean well. Even laws, which by definition are "principles and regulations established by a government and applicable to a people, whether in the form of legislation or of custom and policies recognized and enforced by judicial decision," are constantly up for debate and are reinterpreted at a whim if only for the sake of personal

"Freshly baked" means it arrived frozen and we'll heat it up for you. "Keep out of reach of children" means leave this wherever you want, and if your kids get ahold of it . . . sue.

convenience; though once the law lands where the liberal likes it, it suddenly becomes sacred and immovable.

Only the liberal would consider it "open-minded" to outlaw Nativity scenes in public parks at Christmas so as to make more room for the possibility of an antiglobalization protest parade.

God bless America. Oh wait—is it legal to say that?

☆ 7 ☆

How Liberals Have Created a Nation of Wusses

If the Founding Fathers knew how liberal Americans would abuse our legal system, I believe they would have at least added some kind of amendment to the Constitution that would force all defense lawyers to have to lodge their clients at their homes during the judicial process. If defense lawyers are going to make a living releasing these boneheads on society, the least they can do is get a taste of what they're inflicting on the rest of us when they find themselves being sued by the same societal leeches for being served coffee that was too hot, eggs that were too cold, and orange juice that was too pulpy.

Where do these defense lawyers find these clients, and why are they always getting hurt ten times more often than the rest of us? Put a helmet on 'em before they go out, add shin guards and steel-toed shoes, elbow pads and eye goggles, and . . . ah, forget it. JUST STAY HOME and you won't get hurt.

Every election year a more economically solvent breed of these crybabies runs for office under the "Let's leave a better

Where do defense lawyers find their clients? And why are they always getting hurt ten times more often than the rest of us?

country for our children" platform. What's the problem with this premise? It assumes that the country is in shambles and must be fixed before it's too late. Why else would we elect a guy from another party?

Of course, OUR parents left us nada. I don't know how to break this to you, oh great liberal one, but I think we would end up with a better country if we all lived by the premise "Let's leave a better country to EVERYBODY who's actually still living here now!" I think everyone would be a little more motivated that way.

But the liberal always looks for the lowest common victim, so we all will feel sorry for them, so we won't notice their plan to extort our tax dollars because we made the mistake of getting a job and keeping it. Invoking kids for political gain is easy since everybody has a kid, knows a kid, or was a kid. I say liberals should pick on someone their own size.

Speaking of liberal offspring, I don't understand how liberal parents are able to instill in their kids the ability to be self-sufficient without being self . . . *ish*. The conservative believes that our country was formed on the premise that there is a God in heaven and that he REALLY likes us, which taught kids that they had an obligation to something much bigger and more important than themselves. Once God was removed from schools, kids didn't know where their moral concepts were coming from.

Consequently, the liberal kids stayed in public school in order to get their moral marching orders from secular, unbiased agencies, like NOW and the Rainbow Coalition, and neo-Darwinian evolutionary theory that teaches kids they come from animals, which begs the question, Why should we be disturbed when they act like them? Conservative kids continued searching for God, and when they found he was no longer in schools, they just did what liberals told them to and kept God at home, which also happened to be where they started their new school. Liberal kids don't get home-schooled because their parents aren't at home; they are off actualizing themselves making as much money as they can in order to be able to hire other people to raise their kids all in the name of leaving a better world for the next generation.

> Neo-Darwinian evolutionary theory teaches kids they come from animals, which begs the question, Why should we be disturbed when they act like them?

Banning God from public institutions placed the liberal in the same boat as the Communists when they tried to instill national allegiance through a human being. China worships the state, North Korea has Kim Jong Il, and liberals in America have recycling in order to make a pleasing sacrifice to Mother Nature.

Of course, when push comes to shove and liberals have to come up with someone to worship in order to prove their spirituality, what would be more obvious than . . . themselves? Self-esteem became the mantra for the postmodern pupil. I must love me first, for if I love me, then I will FEEL good enough about myself to get through the day! Of course, the great problem with a me-oriented population is that self-esteem seems to require daily refreshing, which seems to me to be a tremendous expense of time and energy, and means that the rest of us have to kowtow to every whim of the esteemee whenever he's feeling inadequate. This so-called esteem movement has left us with a bunch of kids who are spineless cowards, like in H. G. Wells's *The Time Machine*—kids who'd let the Morlochs eat their brethren because they lost the memory of how to be strong in the midst of difficulty and willingly exchanged safety for freedom.

Once again, liberals start with a false and erroneous idea that consequently fails to properly guide their reasoning through the caverns of truth. Conservatives have always gone with the tried-and-true Judeo-Christian ethic that believes that God gives one purpose and self-esteem. The conservative thinks we are inherently bad and, through careful thought, hard work, and God's blessing, we'll spend our days trying to be good. Isn't this rather self-evident, based on what went down in the Garden of Eden? The liberal, on the other hand, thinks humans are inherently good. Liberals don't seem to comprehend the fact that you don't have to take time to teach your kids how to be selfish; *selfishness comes naturally*. We have to teach them how to share! We don't need to train our kids how to hit other kids; we need to train them how not to whale on a bully even when you want to, and he really, really deserves it.

This self-esteem thing has gone so far over the top that we have ended up with a farce of what was once a noble breed of Americans. "Johnny can't tie his shoe! Oh, let's not force him into learning to tie his shoe in case it puts too much pressure on him; I don't want him to lose his self-esteem. I know, let's put Velcro straps on Johnny's shoe, which will make him feel better until he's in high school and needs to tie a knot and won't know how. Then what will we do about his self-esteem!" Or, "Johnny wants to play on the monkey bars—but what if he slips and falls down, hurts his knee, and then, worse, feels ashamed because all his classmates are laughing at him? I know, let's remove the monkey bars altogether so NO ONE can play on them, and if we have to, let's coat them in some kind of cancer-causing rubber sealant so at least no one can scrape themselves . . . Oh, yes, and let's also install soft padding on the ground so in case he falls he'll bounce."

We had monkey bars. Remember what was beneath them? ASPHALT!

Then there is the pièce de résistance in the Culture of Wusses that the liberals have created: the antibacterial wipe. How have we survived as a species until now without the antibacterial wipe? God forbid, kids today get a germ inside them. Not a germ! No wonder we have a multibillion-dollar antibiotic industry. The real problem is, we don't let ENOUGH germs get inside our kids so their bodies can learn to fight them off the way God intended!

If you really love your kids, the next time they drop a sucker in the dirt, pick it up, blow it off, and shove it back in their mouths the way our moms used to. And if you *really* need an antibacterial wipe, spit on a Kleenex and wipe their faces! That was our antibacterial wipe . . . and look how we turned out.

☆ 8 ☆

I'm Protesting Your Gun Ban

One of the ideas in the Constitution that makes liberals loco is the Second Amendment. You know, the one that gives us the right to keep and bear arms. Only a liberal could turn the First Amendment's free exercise of religion into religious repression while interpreting the right to bear arms as the Founding Fathers' intentions to ban them. Nothing so inflames the liberal orthodoxy than their inability to convince the rest of us that machines are inherently evil. Not people, mind you, machines.

That's what a gun is, after all. An invention created by man with which to defend himself and hunt. The fact that we created guns with this express purpose is still not enough evidence for the liberal to put any blame of misuse on the possessor of the firearm. They always believe the best way to control gun misuse and possible accidental death and dismemberment is to ban guns altogether.

But this plays right into the premise that conservative minds clearly understand and that liberal minds are apparently unable to grasp: "Guns don't kill people . . . bullets kill people!" If a bullet is in a chamber, somebody put it there. If they put it there, they knew what could happen if the gun was accidentally fired. If they put it there with an intent to kill and then shot somebody, it means they KNEW what they were doing and chose to do it anyway! So, in my book, that doesn't make them insane, it makes them evil, and they should be punished accordingly.

But let's be clear about one thing: The gun had no say in this matter. It just exists, as it is, until a cognitive brain makes the decision to utilize it. Somehow, liberal minds believe that by banning guns they can force humans to act in a way that is most beneficial to society. Expecting people to alter their behavior is out of the question to the liberal since they are apparently unconvinced that one's internal law of right and wrong will guide them to the right conclusion. It makes *much* more sense to simply alter our options by trying to impose more laws that limit our freedom and act as a default moral standard. That way no one gets hurt!

Maybe I'm crazy, but I am not reassured by this allusion of goodness, whereby people aren't actually more civilized because they know better but pretend to be more civilized simply because they don't have ready access to a potentially lethal machine. Banning allows the liberal to believe that he has made the world a better place simply because he deludes himself into thinking that if a potentially dangerous item doesn't exist, evil people won't look to find another option by which to harm us. Give me an example of when banning anything actually worked. We tried to ban liquor once in this country. Oh, that worked like a charm. No one could find a drink in the Roaring Twenties! Cuban imports were banned, yet you would have to hire someone to help you find a guy in America who hasn't smoked a Cuban cigar. And the few attempts at banning books never led to the books being unavailable; a ban simply guaranteed that the author would make a boatload of money on it, which enabled him to hopefully write another bannable book. There's just something about banning that seems to guarantee a banned item's attractiveness, of course defeating the purpose of the ban altogether.

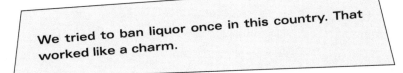

We tried to ban liquor once in this country. That worked like a charm.

Where I live, guns are actually passed down from father to son, and the kids are taught how to respect and use them properly through hunting and target shooting. But I realize male bonding with a firearm is something that only conservative-minded men can appreciate, and is probably similar to the liberal-minded father taking his son to his first seminar in learning how to get in touch with his feminine side.

As a conservative, I, too, wish that no one would ever again die because of a handgun. But since criminals will ALWAYS have them, I think it's crucial for innocent civilians to have the option to defend themselves. But that's just me. Since liberals believe banning works so well, maybe we should cut to the chase, and instead of banning guns, let's just ban crime.

I'm surprised Harry Reid and Ted Kennedy haven't already authored a bill.

☆ 9 ☆

Keep Your Censors Off My Chopsticks

I once walked into a Chinese restaurant to eat some Chinese food. Ah, the Chinese, where would we be without them? I love Chinese food, and I respect the traditional Chinese culture. They have invented many wonderful things, from abacuses to gunpowder—stuff we need. Think of how less dramatic the Fourth of July would have been had the Chinese not invented gunpowder! We would have had to settle for rockets that just sat on the ground and didn't move, not nearly the motivation we would have needed to pack the kids up and take them to the park to watch a spectacular fireworks display. So, I am a China fan!

But when it comes to eating Chinese food in America, I'm afraid they're going to have to make some concessions. I went into this restaurant to eat, and the waiter gave me chopsticks. Now that's OK, since it was a Chinese restaurant, but I politely told him that I don't know *how* to use chopsticks, so I was going to need some silverware.

They didn't have any.

This is where I got a little testy. First of all, look at me. (Turn to front cover.) Do I look like someone who should be proficient with chopsticks? At the risk of being "insensitive"—which has never stopped me before—I'm just pointing out the obvious. No other ethnic restaurant I have ever been in has ever *expected* me to master their traditions in order to eat my meal. I have never gone into an Italian restaurant and had a waiter say, "OK, here's your spaghetti . . . but first! . . . play the mandolin." NEVER! Every other restaurant I've been in has offered me a knife, a fork, and a spoon. (You know why, because we figured out a couple thousand years ago that cutlery is an upgrade from STICKS!)

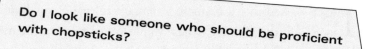

Do I look like someone who should be proficient with chopsticks?

So I asked the manager (politely), "Why isn't there any silverware?"

He replied, "We don't have silverware because we want to be authentic!"

That was it.

"Oh, so you want to be authentic! OK, let me get this straight . . . BOB. I just walked into a Chinese restaurant in a strip mall in the United States of America. I entered through brushed-aluminum and glass doors. I was greeted by a blonde girl who led me to my Formica table and handed me a plastic laminated menu. I'm about to order Chinese food cooked by that Mexican guy in the back, and when I finish I'm going to pay with a credit card, but you think if you throw in some chopsticks, suddenly, I'll think I've been transported into the Ming dynasty! What fictional land are you living in? I'm afraid if you're going to want me to participate in your fantasy world, you're going to have to give me a moment to prepare to suspend my disbelief. I'm going to have to get ready to enter into the 'I reject all modern technology' role-playing theme day that I was unaware was a prerequisite to eating in your place. Next time I'll wake up to the sound of a rooster outside my open window. I'll get up and look in the backyard at my sundial to see what time it is. Then I'll take my clothes down to the nearest stream and beat them with a rock to get them nice and clean! I'll call my girl up to see if she wants to eat out tonight, but I won't use a phone, I'll use a telegraph, or, better yet, smoke signals. Then I'll pick her up but not in a car. I'll grab a Roman chariot, or perhaps a rickshaw. Then when we get to your place and finish eating, I won't pay with my credit card, I'll pay with two hens, a handwoven blanket, and some beads. Then when I bring my girl home, I won't just walk her to the door, instead I'll hit her over the head with a club and drag her there by the hair! Then WHEN YOU THROW IN CHOPSTICKS, I'LL GET IT!!!"

I told this joke at a chapel service at Pepperdine University, at one of two shows they had hired me to perform that year. But I was fired after the first show. Because I did the chopsticks joke, the booker said. I found this confusing, since the joke is basically about my incompetence when it comes to using chopsticks as well as my frustration with a ludicrous attempt to bring authenticity to an obviously inauthentic scenario.

But then the crux of the matter revealed itself when the

booker told me my unpardonable sin in doing this joke was the fact that I believe silverware is superior to chopsticks.

My unpardonable sin? I believe silverware is superior to chopsticks.

Now, friends, I always try to be honest with myself when it comes to performing, always try to get better and search for ways to best communicate my ideas. Contrary to how it might appear, I do want to be sensitive to others, so as I analyzed it, and if I was willing to be honest with myself, I had to admit that I did indeed say that silverware was better than chopsticks . . . BECAUSE IT IS!! I'd challenge a liberal to a race. I'll take a spoon, you take chopsticks, here's a bowl of soup, let's see who gets to the bottom first! But the efficiency of flatware was not the point. Apparently, two kids complained about the show, and that was that. I'm not going to risk being politically incorrect by revealing their ethnicity, but you can pretty much rule out that their last names were Rodriguez.

You want an accurate gauge of how mature you are? How easy is it for you to laugh at yourself? Being able to laugh at differences instead of fight about them should be the norm when it comes to the intersection of cultures, which is all America really is. Liberals presuppose that the content of an idea is more important than the context, whereas the conservative is always more concerned about the context of an idea than the content.

After the show (which, of course, contained other topics and bits), a male African American student approached me and said,

"Thanks—it really made me think." Another male, of the melanin-impaired variety, came up to me and said, "I'm a vegan" (the most radical form of vegetarianism), "but I thought your animal-rights material was very funny." A young (I hope I don't offend her) "female" came to me and sardonically said she was going to start wearing fur. Another young "man" (does that sound sexist/elitist to you?) asked if I was a libertarian, and another wanted me to speak to their young Republicans group on campus.

You know what the greatest disappointment about being fired from that gig was? The greatest disappointment was that these were supposed to be *my people*. Pepperdine is a "Christian" university, and yet, when I dared express my opinions, I was accused of being ethnocentric and insensitive and bigoted. Despite the fact that, unsolicited, I had gotten positive feedback from the gamut of races, genders, and ideologies who were paying tuition. The kids themselves were telling me how much they got out of the show, which proved that, through humor, I reached them with the unifying message that I would speak the truth, unfettered, as the First Amendment was designed to allow. Because two kids (of the 150 kids at the chapel) were unable to separate the content of my joke from the context, the entire student body was denied the opportunity to judge me for themselves.

The university's so-called creed of being a forum for free thought and diverse opinion took a nosedive into murky liberal waters, where it's assumed that young adults' minds are too malleable and too easily confused by thoughts and opinions that don't come with anti-American, anti-conservative screed out of the tenured mouths of liberal professors—professors, I might add, who are usually too gutless to live among adults in the real world and instead prefer to have their egos stroked by eighteen-year-olds who've been manipulated into thinking they're geniuses.

I don't call that "sensitivity." I call it "censorship." Shame on you, Pepperdine.

☆ 10 ☆

Gender Neutrality or Transtupidity?

M en and women are different. Who would have thought that statement would ever be up for debate in anything other than a science-fiction novel? Somehow, for reasons I can't begin to comprehend, this concept is insulting to a liberal's way of thinking, presumably because any stated difference allows for the possibility of unfair superiority. (That's why I say men and women are different as often as possible, mainly because liberals tell me I can't, and it makes them furious, which of course makes great sport for me.)

In a perfect example of how highly educated intellectuals with doctoral degrees are often wrong, the psychiatric community in the 1970s experimented with the age-old concept of gender by encouraging parents to give dolls to their boys. Their goal? To prove that cultural indoctrination was the only reason boys wouldn't play with them. "They'd play with them if they weren't made to feel ashamed," the experts said. And they were right. Boys, being boys, pulled off the dolls' heads, pretended to saw them in half with their swords, and dropped them out the window to see if they'd break or bounce—and that was only because they didn't have a magnifying glass with which to burn holes through their skulls.

> Boys, being boys, pulled off the dolls' heads.

Growing up with an older sister gave me plenty of opportunity to notice our physical differences, not to mention become acquainted with the Defending Yourself Double Standard. See, boys are raised (or at least we used to be) to never hit a girl. My mother crammed this concept down my throat, practically chanting, "Never hit a girl, never hit a girl, never never never . . . hit a . . . girl!" I got it (the first time) and considered it sound enough advice until she went to teach my sister how to defend herself. Then, suddenly, my mild-mannered mom turned into a demonic martial arts instructor.

"If a boy bothers you," she'd cackle, "kick him where it counts! Mmmooowhaaa!"

"Kick him where it counts," as though someone's keeping score ("two points . . . THWACK!") was the phrase used in my household to make the heinous act of temporarily maiming a boy's testicles sound less offensive to our young ears. The worst part of it, as you may know, is the fact that kicking a guy in the groin is somehow humorous to a girl. That's right, they find it funny. Anytime a low-budget movie needs a quick laugh, you can almost hear the director whisper, "Hey, just kick 'em in the crotch!"

Once my sister learned this trick, she had the audacity to try to rationalize the pain she'd inflicted. She'd taunt, "It can't hurt that bad, it probably just feels like a girl getting hit in the chest." Uhhh . . . no. Your chest is a gland, and my crotch is an organ. You want to know what it feels like? Pull your eyes out of their sockets, let them hang on your cheeks, and then give 'em a good slap.

This whole concept of exposed organs seems like God's grievous error. Most every other organ in a man's body (heart, lungs, spleen) is protected by his rib cage. What happened? I'll tell you what happened. The one stinking rib God took from Adam to make Eve was the one protecting our crotch! The most blatant disregard for the male anatomy that I can think of at this moment (give me time) is the concept of the "boy's bike." My boy's bike featured a straight stiff steel bar that reached from under my seat to the front of the bike's frame. The first time your feet slipped off the pedals, you were sure you were a boy!! Is it me or did they get the bike design backward?

> The one stinking rib God took from Adam to make Eve was the one protecting our crotch!

But of course, whether the liberal likes to acknowledge it or not, it's true that there are gradations of differences between men and women, as well as gender-based strengths and weaknesses. Take sports. In this day of steroids and weight training, we still don't see a woman playing professional sports alongside men. The fact is, women just aren't as strong or as fast. No doubt bringing up this obvious point will anger many a radical feminist, but the proper response to this fact from anyone with a functioning brain should be, SO WHAT? Our bodies are different, and we excel in different areas of life.

Now, it's my personal opinion that the uniquely God-given superiority that women have over men borders on the supernatural at times, and is far more amazing and useful than men's brute strength—everything from their psychic ability to read a man's mind (especially when he says one thing but obviously means another) to their uncanny ability to spontaneously start crying when confronted with a speeding ticket. If a man even *tried* that on an officer, he would be arrested just because it would be so embarrassingly uncomfortable to watch.

Women also have an impressive ability to locate an item in the refrigerator from twenty feet away:

Us, after five minutes of searching: "Babe, we're out of mayonnaise."

Them, out of eyeshot, from two rooms away: "It's behind the black olives on the third shelf next to the pasta we brought home from Macaroni Grill."

A woman's first response to conflict is different from a man's. Women normally try to assess a situation calmly and reasonably, whereas a man instantly looks for anything with a detonator.

In other words, for lots of reasons, many larger and profound (but not as funny) as these, we need each other. We need each other to help balance out our flaws and foibles. That is exactly what good marriages do.

Of course, pointing out the obvious differences between men and women irritates liberals since they consider these gender-based tendencies "stereotypes." I've got news for them: The reason stereotypes exist is because *they are true!* (If they weren't, there would be no such thing as stand-up comedy.) Gender stereotypes make us laugh because we can all relate to them. No matter what our cultural background, stereotypes speak to us because they describe a common experience—and when it comes to men and women, stereotypes help us to realize we're not alone in our inability to understand the opposite sex (since the truth is, no one does and no one ever will).

Men who are honest with themselves realize that we'd never make it without women. Women reflect the best of us—even God acknowledges this in the Bible when he says man "wasn't complete" until he had a woman alongside him. Obviously, that's why God made man first, so he could practice.

The many and varied differences between men and women are precisely what make marriage holy in the eyes of a religious conservative. It's *because* it's hard to get along that we make sacrifices to demonstrate our love for our spouse. Liberals, once again harkening back to the sixties and seventies, base marriage on the fulfillment of individual needs. If those needs aren't met, you have the right to leave and find "yourself," which changes the game, my friends, from an expectation of working through the hard stuff as lifelong wife/husband, to business partners who sell their shares when things get tough and go form a new company!

What makes me an expert on marriage? I have been married thirteen years. As of yet, I haven't had an affair or considered divorce. Not because marriage is easy, but because it's hard, and the conservative isn't afraid of hard. Hard is good. For me, it conjures up that old idiom that needs to be resurrected and handed to every son, brother, and boy you meet on the street: Be a man. I'm proud of my unique manhood and make no apologies for it, whether the liberal likes it or not.

I'm also grateful for my wife and am man enough to admit I need her: "Desiree . . . where's the mayonnaise?"

☆ 11 ☆

How Jesus Teaches Tolerance

One of the lessons I've learned as a comedian who is an open conservative and an out-of-the-closet Christian is that if you believe something that limits liberal choice or belief, you're a bigot. If a liberal, on the other hand, tries to limit a conservative's choice, they're progressive. And while many liberals are smart people (believe it or not), most are unable to recognize that when they call a conservative closed-minded or intolerant, they're being closed-minded and intolerant themselves!

Let me show you what passes for "tolerance" in the liberal world. I once was on a television show in which I made the statement that I believe humans only have two purposes in life. First is to know God, second is to share with others that you found him. Within the context of this statement, I, a Christian man, repeated an idea that goes along with the orthodoxy of the religion I accept as truth. I said that "some people will never know God, and they will go to hell. Others will find him but not give their life back to him." Because of that statement, I received a mean-spirited e-mail from a liberal, telling me in no uncertain terms how offended she was by my remarks. (I always save mean-spirited e-mails so that I can use them as specimens in my show, one of the many perks of being a stand-up comedian!)

She defined my remarks as "narrow-minded" and "bigoted." Good thing liberals come from a place of compassion and tolerance! Remember, the most important thing the liberal wants to get across to you is that she is offended. In the Bible of Liberal Thought, to be offended is the ultimate sin, and it always comes with the assumption that we are supposed to CARE that they are offended. As much as I am in search of common ground, as a conservative, I know the only way to deal with this type of liberal rhetorical tactic is to not cave. If getting along in society is predicated on having to cower in a corner every time the liberal mind cries, "You hurt my feelings!" then we have gone from a society of free thought to a society of imprisoned intellect.

I could understand her being offended if I (or my religion) came from a place of coercion. But I never tell people they must believe like me or I will make them eat meat and watch reruns of *The Facts of Life*. But saying, "Believe in Jesus or someday God will judge your decision" is my First Amendment right and shouldn't bother anyone, *especially* if they disbelieve the premise. It's like the atheist who wants "under God" removed from the Pledge of Allegiance because it "offends" him. Dude, you're an atheist! You don't even believe in God, how can he offend you? Who is more irrational, the guy who believes in a God he can't see, or a guy who's offended by a God he doesn't believe in?

The fact is, Jesus was a controversial character, and he's still ruffling feathers to this day. Even if you *believe* the story of

I never tell people they must believe like me or I will make them eat meat and watch reruns of *The Facts of Life*.

His deity to be true, as I do, it STILL makes for a big leap of faith, so I can almost (almost) understand the dissension and disbelief among our non-Christian brethren. Think about it: Jesus claimed that he was God. That's a big one to swallow. He was God for thirty-three years, and yet he only told people about it for three! Don't you think his friends had to suspect something? Come on, everyone goes to the beach, they're swimming, and there's Jesus—*walking on the water*. All his friends could do was stare in disbelief and say, "No wonder he never brings a towel."

Jesus was God for thirty-three years, yet he only told people about it for three. Don't you think his friends had to suspect something? Everyone goes to the beach, and there's Jesus—*walking on the water*.

People would go on picnics, and Jesus would show up empty-handed, borrow a couple of fish and a few loaves of bread, and voilá, plenty for everyone. Then, there's the fact that Jesus had brothers and sisters. Can you imagine being the brother of Jesus?

You wouldn't get away with anything! Mary comes home from a long day at the market, and says:

"OK, who broke my new clay vessel? . . . John!"

"Oh sure, Mom, it always has to be me, doesn't it? Oh, it couldn't be Jesus, could it, nooo . . . he's . . . perfect! . . ." (The one time he did break something, Jesus healed it before she got home.)

So, yes, I will admit, the whole religion concept is not easy to believe, but I didn't call Jesus the Messiah, he did!

Now, my conservative brethren, in responding to my pen pal, I simply used the same rhetorical attacks she used on me. This acts like kryptonite on the liberal-minded. Supposedly, the ultimate goal of the liberal is to be tolerant of others' personal beliefs, but tolerance can't come at the price of compromising personal convictions or they are no longer convictions but "subjective opinions." What I am most proud of is the fact that by the end of our communication, we were actually finding common ground, even though our positions never changed.

What makes our country great is not that everyone agrees. What makes our country great is how civilly we can disagree. That is why conservative minds must always be prepared intellectually to defend their point of view, and if you don't . . . you're going to hell.

☆ 12 ☆

Why Conservatives Love Wal-Mart (and Liberals Love the State of Taxes)

I love Wal-Mart. The size . . . the selection . . . the vests. Even the smell, a distinct bouquet combining the fresh scent of thousands of deodorants paired with the pungent aroma of brand-new tires, makes Wal-Mart, hands down, the best store there ever was. It's a conservative American's mecca, and every shopping day is our pilgrimage.

I'm amazed by the whiners coming out of the woodwork (which, by the way, they could have gotten cheaper at Wal-Mart) condemning Wal-Mart as the "evil corporate giant." Leave it to the liberal to be angry at Wal-Mart for having the audacity to be better at business than everybody else. My thinking is, if you hate Wal-Mart, you hate capitalism, so do us all a favor and move to North Korea, where you can experience the freedom of never owning your own business!

It's hard for me to wrap my mind around exactly what a liberal could find to complain about at Wal-Mart. It provides enough jobs to equal the GNP of most nations. It sells the best products to people like . . . oh, I don't know . . . ME, for example, cheaper than anyone else. Any store that makes it a policy to stock not just the products you love but *every product manufactured on the face of this planet* is as capitalist as it gets. Where else can you buy a complete wardrobe and place settings for six for less than five bucks?

It's hard for me to wrap my mind around exactly what a liberal could find to complain about at Wal-Mart. Where else can you buy a complete wardrobe and place settings for six for less than five bucks?

I think what really drives liberals out of their minds is that Middle America invented Wal-Mart, while the liberals were too busy creating the Internet. The big liberal babies cry, "Yeah, but Wal-Mart destroys all the mom-and-pop stores in small communities." I don't know how to break it to them, the great masters of impaired analytic reasoning, but Wal-Mart *started* as a mom-and-pop store! Mom and Pop Walton just did it better than Abbie Hoffman's mom and pop. Liberals are just jealous that it wasn't *their* mom and pop who succeeded in creating a $12-billion-a-year business.

The truth is, the liberal only likes Monopoly when he can control Boardwalk and Park Place. But, unlike most liberals, at least Wal-Mart is philanthropic in its investment into its communities. *Forbes* magazine recently recognized Wal-Mart as the nation's top corporate cash giver—they donate over $200 million to charities every year. They give greeter jobs to old people who would be saying hi to you for free in the mall. Now, I'm not saying Wal-Mart's perfect, or that I agree with everything they do (I'm not crazy about their buying so many products from China, mainly because I'm not crazy about the way China treats its dissenters). But there is something about this arrogant tendency liberals have to think somehow it's their job to dictate to the rest of us how to behave and how to spend our *own* money. If liberals had created Wal-Mart, I guarantee they would be extolling its virtues. Then, about a week later, the business would go under due to their inability to say no to employees who demanded two months' paid vacation and a livable wage of fifty bucks an hour.

The truth is, the liberal only likes Monopoly when he can control Boardwalk and Park Place.

If a conservative employee of a private company doesn't like the way he's treated, he . . . quits. (The liberal who wants a company that gives him everything he could wish for—including self-esteem—irrespective of his qualifications, should apply to the Democratic Party.) For whatever reason, liberals are somehow incapable of acknowledging that there will always be gradations of income. Some people will always have more than others, and that's good. If there were no rich people, where would the money to help the poor people come from? Remember, we're Americans: The possibility of making more for you and yours is supposed to be an incentive. What was that old saying, "A BMW is the mother of invention"?

The liberal maintains that rich people are evil and always acquire their money by exploiting the poor. As punishment for the deed of becoming rich, they maintain that the rich should have to pay more taxes than those of us who aren't. And yet, very strangely, I have never met a liberal in a high-profile, powerful position who wasn't rich. So, let's add it up: Liberal Democrats claw their way into office in part to raise taxes, especially those targeting the rich. Except it's the liberal who *is* rich.

Maybe I'm crazy, but anyone who looks at his portfolio and proclaims, "The only thing missing here is that I'm not paying enough taxes!" is an idiot! I don't ever want a guy running the country who WANTS to pay more taxes, even if it is because his own tax burden is softened by the same means that he and all his golf buddies have at their disposal (tax shelters, paid health insurance, limos with drivers, free five-star dinners, speaking engagements for ridiculous sums of money, book deals, and corporate contributions). And what's it all for? To get famous, powerful, and rich, so they can create more opportunities to tell poor people how bad rich people are! None of which makes any sense, since the only thing most poor people want is to not be poor anymore.

I don't ever want a guy running the country who WANTS to pay more taxes, even if it is because his own tax burden is softened by the same means that he and all his golf buddies have at their disposal.

I don't believe in penalizing the wealthy for committing the sin of achievement. I do believe in helping those less fortunate, but in the form of charities, churches, and other private organizations whose very purpose is to provide for the downtrodden. How many millions of dollars must be wasted before the liberal wakes up to the reality that when the government is put in charge of philanthropy, it's just not going to be effective? We need to continue to allow the conservative work ethic to lead and inspire our children. It works because it comes with the expectation of reward for the effort put forth. People come to America to get rich, and even if they don't, the fact that the possibility is just around the corner is enough for them to stay, or to leave everything behind, wherever they are, to pursue the American dream.

The conservative way is to leave the money in the pockets of those who earned it. As an American, I want to choose how to spend the money I've rightfully earned. I'll pay my taxes, and if I get rich, that's a testament to God's blessing, hard work, and my country's free-market potential.

Now, if you'll excuse me, I need to get to Wal-Mart to get a hot dog and some mascara. (I don't usually wear mascara, but at these prices, I can't afford *not* to!)

☆ 13 ☆

One Nation, in Air Travel

As Americans, we're used to being allowed to travel any-where we want, anytime we want, the only restriction being the occasional hemorrhoidal flare-up. Travel means freedom, and, harkening back to those early covered-wagon days, our her-itage.

The irony is that, contrary to this birthright, I've always been afraid to fly, which is no small obstacle for a guy who makes his living touring about a hundred cities each year. And, so, while I was still afraid to fly (only with bigger, scarier reasons), air travel in those first few days after the terrorists attack was in some ways a comfort to me. *Everyone* was so stunned and confused, I could finally be scared to fly and nobody would make fun of me! Strangely, I found myself longing for the days when the only thing you had to be afraid of when you flew was crashing. Now, I have to worry about the guy next to me lighting his shoe on fire. Who's training these terrorists? Maxwell Smart?

Strangely, the airlines have never acknowledged our fear of

Who's training these terrorists? Maxwell Smart?

flying. Why not? Man, being created without wings, clearly wasn't *supposed* to fly, but good old industrious Americans like Orville and Wilbur Wright just figured it out one day, kudos to us. I want to fly an honest airline with a crew that says stuff like, "Have a great flight . . . you'll probably make it!"

"Truth" is the buzzword for traditional Americans like me. Let us know what we're in for—no really, we want to know—and we'll take it from there. Look, I'm thirty thousand feet in the air traveling five hundred miles an hour, and I'm being driven by a pilot one can only hope isn't on Thorazine. There is a risk here, so we may as well just admit it, then we're all in the same boat. That's the American spirit that got us this far.

Instead of telling it like it is, liberals patronize us with irrelevant stats that are supposed to make us feel better: "It's safer to fly in a plane than to drive in a car . . ." Yeah, well, it's also safer to CRASH in a car than it is in a plane! THAT'S the stat that matters! You get in a car wreck, they say, "Anybody hurt?" Get in a plane wreck, they say "Anybody RECOGNIZABLE?" Car wreck, you're a vegetable; plane wreck, you're a mineral.

It's safer to CRASH in a car than it is in a plane. THAT'S the stat that matters! Car wreck, you're a vegetable; plane wreck, you're a mineral.

The hypocrisy of the airlines is stunning. Don't be afraid to fly, they say, yet the first thing they teach you on a plane is how to crash. They don't teach crash techniques when you get on a bus or train, they just figure you'll improvise. On a plane, they teach you to protect yourself in the event of a crash by putting your head down and placing your hands over your head. Like this will keep me from blowing up! *This* makes you invincible? If it's that effective, I'm going to use it in all life-threatening situations. Some guy tries to mug me, waving a gun in my face? I'm bending over with hands on my head.

We're not supposed to be afraid to fly, meanwhile they're pointing out all these exit signs to "be aware of" in case of a wreck. "We have exits everywhere, one in front, two in the rear, and two over the wings." Exits over the wing? If we've crashed, chances are, that's probably what came off.

Even the plane's design is suspicious. Everything doubles for something else. My seat's a flotation device? Who's designing this plane, Salvador Dalí? Pardon me, but I've yet to see someone drowning and the lifeguard screaming, "Throw him a chair!" The next thing you know, they'll be telling me that my barf bag doubles as scuba gear.

My favorite part of plane preparation? After they've explained every possible life-and-death situation that could occur and expect you to be clear-headed enough after this forty-five seconds of training to qualify as a Navy SEAL . . . after we've been asked to think of normal items like seat cushions and barf bags in innovative and lifesaving ways . . . they demo *how to buckle your seat belt*. If you were born and raised in the United States and don't know how to work a seat belt, you are a burden on society. Making it an FAA regulation to demo a seat belt is so dumb it

HAD to be a liberal idea, if for no other reason than to invent a needless job with the title "pre-takeoff meandering tripe rhetoric writer" so somebody unqualified to do anything meaningful could make residuals on their alleged wordsmithery.

> Making it an FAA regulation to demo a seat belt is so dumb it HAD to be a liberal idea, if for no other reason than to invent a needless job.

So I was terrified to fly (just as the terrorists had hoped) but I finally decided, if I died in the air, I died for my country. Unlike the terrorists, I come from a belief system that doesn't force people to believe in it. So, if I died, I died for my God. I realized that, as an American, I was lucky to be born free, and freedom (if you're a conservative) means making choices and being responsible for what happens to you. I realized if I gave in to the fear, I would not be teaching my kids that there are things in life more important than life, and so if I died, I would have died standing for a principle I believed in: I would have died for my family.

Three conservative ideals—God, country, and family.

If you have nothing worth dying for, you have nothing worth living for. So I got on that plane. Every soldier starts out a civilian; it was my turn to risk something for freedom.

Score one for the Americans . . . now where's my Dramamine?

☆ 14 ☆

Beware Blind Terrorists in Wheelchairs

On September 11, 2001, terrorist freaks tried to steal more from America than just our innocence. They also tried to steal our joy of travel. If there is one thing the terrorists got right in judging America's resolve, it wasn't that we wouldn't retaliate to defend ourselves, it was our defense against inconvenience. Make us pay upward of two dollars for a gallon of gas, or get to the airport two hours early? Now you've gone too far.

It's amazing how air travel has changed since September 11. When I was nine and flew with my grandpa on my first airplane ride from Indiana to California to start my new life, plane travel was still exotic. Men wore suits, women wore dresses, I wore a dickey with a sweater vest, and the stewardesses* were commanded to be attractive. If there is any profession where the idea of tenure just isn't working, it's being a stewardess. Give them

*Back in my day, stewardesses were called stewardesses. Today, they want to be called flight attendants, which is the politically correct term espoused by liberals and exactly the reason why I'm not calling them that. Touché, First Amendment.

their retirement and let them go home, *please*. (They are in a profession where they have to be stared at for hours at a time; nobody needs that kind of scrutiny at sixty plus. Trust me, when I get old, I'll live off my album residuals 'cause the entertainment biz doesn't need another Keith Richards.)

When I was nine and flew with my grandpa on my first airplane ride, plane travel was still exotic. Men wore suits, women wore dresses, I wore a dickey with a sweater vest.

Another glaring difference between flying today and flying back then was there weren't even metal detectors at airports. You just walked straight to the gate. All you had on you was maybe a carry-on and a shotgun, and the security process went something like this:

"Sir, is that loaded?"

"Yeah."

"Well, is the safety on?"

"Yes, ma'am."

It was a simpler time, a time when people were naive enough to believe that no one in their right mind would blow up a plane that they were *still in*!

"Well, c'mon in!"

Even armed and loaded, they trusted you! It was a simpler time, a time when people were naive enough to believe that no one in their right mind would blow up a plane that they were *still in*! Ah, the innocence . . .

Nobody thinks of an airport as fun anymore because, frankly, it isn't. There *was* a time when going to the airport was the first step of an adventure: "We're going to Grandma's house!" Or, in my family, "Grandma's going home!" It's still an event, but there's something about being frisked by a stranger, taunted by the artificial aroma of Cinnabon, and threatened by automatic weapons that has somehow undermined the allure. Everybody's so serious and uptight, especially, of course, the security people.

If there is a profession that is least appreciated at the airport it's that of a professional comedian. Take it from me, folks, save yourself the inconvenience of an anal probe and don't try to joke with these people because they have no sense of humor. There are things you just shouldn't do at the airport no matter how much fun it would be for everyone else in line. For example, if a security person asks if they can look through your luggage, do not say, "Sure," while holding your hands over your ears and diving under the table. Do not lie on the conveyor belt and go through the X-ray machine. (They're used to seeing purses and laptops, not skeletons, and they HATE that.)

However we Americans might be inconvenienced, it didn't take the ACLU guy two minutes to make sure that our security measures would in no way inconvenience those who might *look* like terrorists. I'm referring to the oh-so-effective "no profiling" rule. Boy, has that made security more rational. No matter how

German I'm looking on any particular day, they want to check my luggage. Of course, I am singled out exactly BECAUSE I look nothing like the people who attacked us on our soil. The liberal mind conjectures that by choosing people for inspection who obviously don't fit the profile, we're being fair.

> No matter how German I'm looking on any particular day, security wants to check my luggage.

Profiling is something that the liberal mind sees only as detrimental and invasive. Their desire to respect others' personal privacy is completely illogical. They are downright giddy in their enthusiasm to search someone like me (blond, Anglo, clearly American), but err on the side of sensitivity in *not* searching someone who looks very much like the people we know for a fact blew up our buildings and killed our people. *Those* people should be handled with care and left alone *just in case* they're innocent. The heck with common sense.

Liberals will always err on the side of anything BUT America. That is why I believe we need oversensitivity training courses to undo the damage done by sensitivity training. Or we could just maintain the status quo, staying vigilant and respectful, keeping a sharp eye out for the ninety-year-old blind lady who's on oxygen and in a wheelchair because *she* seems a little suspicious.

At least we're not profiling.

☆ 15 ☆

I'm Fat/Sick/Injured,
and It's Your Fault!

Part of my annoyance with the liberal influence on American society is the "blame others for your problems" syndrome they've elevated to new heights. If you're fat, sue McDonald's. If you shoot someone, sue the gun manufacturer. If you get into an accident, sue the car manufacturer. It's epitomized by the poor guy in a neck brace who's dazed by the fact that, in this world, it's actually possible for something to go wrong. (He obviously wasn't wearing his helmet.)

This liberal idea of utopianism that posits that the world is perfect until a corporation decides to build a product is so beyond what America used to stand for that it seems impossible for the liberal to find his way back to a place of reason. Take cars. Do liberals really believe that cars aren't potentially dangerous? "I crashed and somebody must pay!" is the liberal mantra. "Yeah, but you were going ninety around that turn" is the reasonable conservative response. "I know, but they should have created some kind of pogo stick device that shoots out of the sides and bounces me off the Jersey barrier!"

It's amazing how liberals try to appeal to others' decency with what they consider reasonable arguments like, "We live in the United states of America, the most technologically advanced country of all time. We have put men on the moon. Why can't we make the things we run into . . . SOFTER."

If you find yourself constantly looking for reasons why your life isn't where you wish it was, and spend most of your time looking everywhere but at yourself . . . you have been affected by the liberal mind-set that has trained you to look first for excuses and second for a trial attorney. Liberals live in a world of unrealistic expectations. Just exactly where is the dividing line between actual corporate irresponsibility and the assumption that one can conduct his life without being a complete idiot?

> If you find yourself constantly looking for reasons why your life isn't where you wish it was, you have been affected by the liberal mind-set that has trained you to look first for excuses and second for a trial attorney.

If you have ever watched TV in the wee hours of the morning, you probably have seen the ads for "the Accident Attorney." These people have so completely lost the perspective of common sense that they have created a world where the only victim of crime or an accident is the person who commits it.

The ad usually looks and sounds so outlandish at first that

you think you're watching a sketch from a low-budget comedy show. It goes something like this: "Have you been in an accident? Were you drinking under the influence? Do you have a suspended license? Are you in this country illegally? Were you driving a stolen car or found on the wrong side of the road? Don't worry, you have rights! Call me, the Accident Attorney, at 1-800-COP-OUTS, and I will fight for you!"

What is both telling and insulting about these amoral abusers of the justice system is they do this under the guise of having a heart for the perpetrator. And yet, you don't see them making similar outrageous statements that would amount to, "Convicted sex offender? Just out of prison? Carry loaded weapons? Enjoy child pornography? Have you considered a job in the fast-growing market of day care?"

Every time a convicted murderer is let out of prison by a liberal judge because he (and it's usually a he) finally got rehabilitated through that tried-and-true method of "good behavior" at the state penitentiary, you can be sure that the victim of the crime wasn't related to the all-powerful judge. Most judges start out as attorneys, and today, even the best law schools subscribe to the idea that the guilt of a criminal is less important than his attorney's courtroom skills. These judges put more passion into the letter of the law than the real, flesh-and-blood, grieving family sitting in the courtroom with them.

This is the same mind-set that awards hundreds of millions of dollars to "victims" of cancer who *chose* to smoke for forty years but have now *decided* that having only one lung and living on a ventilator may not have been worth the cost of all those enjoyable cigarettes, even the ones with the smooth menthol taste! (Funny how liberals want to afford you the right to kill yourself, but not if it's through a behavioral choice like smoking. No, in that case, they must save you from yourself by condemning the companies that make cigarettes. But the companies that create the drug used for your "dignified" overdose? That one's good! Let's buy stock!)

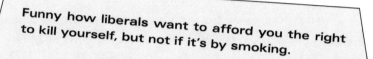

Funny how liberals want to afford you the right to kill yourself, but not if it's by smoking.

The liberal logic (which is an oxymoron): Good is decided by your perspective alone. Which becomes somewhat inconvenient when the you is Jeffrey Dahmer.

☆ 16 ☆

Merry Halloween

I miss the days when Christmas was a holiday everyone celebrated, regardless of their personal religious beliefs. People used to say "Merry Christmas" in the streets, remember that? Of course you don't, because we don't say it anymore. People would cheerily yell it out across the street to neighbors of all kinds, AND they would return the good cheer with their own "Merry Christmas!" Back then, EVERYBODY said "Merry Christmas," because it wasn't about being Christian, it was about unity—once a year, Americans believed that giving to each other also meant that everyone could appreciate the sentiment and not be offended.

Much to my dismay and that of most Christians I know, "Merry Christmas" has been replaced with the watered-down, bland "Happy holidays," which is a catchall for any possible fringe belief you have decided to manufacture. (The only thing that's worse than "Happy holidays" is "Season's greetings.") So now, most Americans in the cowardly tradition of standing up for everyone else's issue but their own say, *"Happy holidays, because I don't want to say 'Christmas' in case you don't believe in Christmas!"*

Trust me, I don't follow in those footsteps. I say "Merry Christmas" to everyone I meet. It's especially gratifying if they are walking out of an ACLU fund-raiser. Try it.

> I say "Merry Christmas" to everyone I meet. It's especially gratifying if they are walking out of an ACLU fund-raiser.

The whole "Happy holidays" premise is, of course, inherently flawed because we are allowed to call a holiday by its proper name, so long as it's not Christian. Look at February. There are a bunch of holidays in February, and no one is panicked by being potentially insulting. No one says "Happy Valentine's Day" followed by, "Oh, sorry, do you believe in love? Are you lonely or alone or unhappy in your relationship? Whoops!"

So what I really want to know is: Which part of the Christmas spirit is more offensive, "Peace on earth" or "Goodwill toward men"? The sad truth is that people don't want to say "Merry Christmas" because "Christmas" contains the word "Christ" (it's his stinkin' birthday, after all), and after two thousand years, he's still intimidating people. Granted, I am a follower so maybe I'm a bit biased, but I'll make you a deal: You show me a more moral man than Jesus, and I'll follow him. Show me another belief system that tells people they have to love your (now get this) ENEMY! Show me the other religion that had the impudence to tell people to "pray for those that despitefully use you."

That is why the Founding Fathers decided that not only could the grand experiment of democracy not work without religion, it would be the Christian religion that we would use as the template for our laws and mores. That's not some kind of oppressive manipulation of history to try to shove my belief down your throat (like a liberal would). *That is the historical truth,* documented hundreds of times over. That is the foundation of America! It's because Christianity became our moral judge that we ARE able to allow diverse religions and philosophies to coexist, side by side, in this great country.

But for those of you out there who are so disgusted by the ridiculous idea that Christmas has anything of value to offer humanity, fear not, your holiday is coming.

You know what the second most popular holiday in the United States is?

Halloween. Let's weigh these two equally joyous holidays, shall we? With one, we get peace on earth, goodwill toward men. With the other, we get . . . BOO!!! By the way, have you noticed that "boo" is the only scare word we know? If we didn't have the word "boo," we would just jump out of the closet and stare at each other.

Let's weigh Christmas and Halloween. With one, we get peace on earth, goodwill toward men. With the other, we get . . . BOO!!!

I don't celebrate Halloween, as it, too, is an inherently flawed holiday, at least in its modern incarnation. Here's how it's supposed to work: Kids walk up to your door and say, "Trick or treat," which means I tricked you, now you have to give me candy. The problem is . . . YOU DIDN'T TRICK ME, because you always come on the SAME DAY. The only way trick or treat would work nowadays is if you came in . . . MAY . . . at three o'clock in the morning and shouted, "Trick or treat!" Then I'd say, "Hey, you got me, here's a pickle."

But even a truly pagan holiday like Halloween is offensive to some liberals. There is a school in Washington that doesn't allow the kids to dress up like witches and goblins because they don't want to offend the local Wicca chapter. (OK, now pick yourself up off the floor and we'll try to keep moving.) This may be an extreme example, but the liberal mind often makes the fatal mistake of being incapable of differentiating between respecting the rights of others who have a different point of view and actually giving that point of view an equally valid place in the real world of ideas. How someone who considers herself an actual witch (which is a whole other topic) would be offended by someone wearing a scary-looking witch mask and striped stockings does a grave disservice to the validity of her belief system, I

How anyone who considers herself an actual witch would be offended by someone wearing a scary-looking mask and striped stockings, I don't know.

don't know. Seriously, if she's that offended, why doesn't she cast a spell and turn the kids into frogs or something?

Anyone who claims they can control or manipulate nature by magic potions and spells would, I think, have a lot bigger fish to fry than being concerned about the spooky power of little children in costume in search of a Kit Kat bar.

☆ 17 ☆

Don't Kill Me 'Cause I'm Short

The sad state of affairs in the United States in the twenty-first century is "the first one out of the womb . . . wins." The debate usually works its way around the fact that the newly conceived zygote is only the size of a pinhead. So, apparently, the idea is that if you're really, REALLY small, you don't deserve the constitutional right to exist without our approval.

This is the most disingenuous element in the abortion debate. Everybody seems to agree that one's body is one of the most important things that exists. This list used to include God (until liberals outlawed him), country (until the liberals became afraid that patriotism made us appear arrogant to the rest of the world), and family (which they are in the process of redefining). But we're at loggerheads when it comes to agreeing how much freedom to give people with respect to how their bodies behave and what they're allowed to do. This places the liberal in an inescapable conundrum, because if you have the right to do what you please with your body, and that right cannot be violated, then to be consistent, that means everyone is allowed this same right—including the zygote/fetus.

The abortion debate always revolves around the fact that women have an inalienable right to absolute autonomy, to make the choice that's best for their bodies. But abortion isn't about what a woman does to her body. It's about what she is allowed to do to the body that's trapped INSIDE of hers!

The double standard—or maybe it's more accurate to call it the doublespeak—is that there are abortion rights ethicists who actually propagate the idea that a baby isn't a baby until the mother decides she wants it. Now, I say if the parent of a yet-to-be-born child is given the exalted position of determining when this human is viable, why limit it? Why can't we carry this through until they leave our household? It makes the choice of "inside the womb" seem almost arbitrary. If, as parents, we could decide to eliminate our kids when and if they become inconvenient, I say we are ending the argument too soon! The question shouldn't be, "Can we eliminate our kids at sixteen weeks?" It would be much more helpful if we could have the option to end their existence at sixteen years! Trust me, there are a lot more parents who find their kids inconvenient at this age. Even if we couldn't *actually* abort them in their teens, the sug-

> If, as parents, we could decide to eliminate our kids when and if they become inconvenient, it would be much more helpful to end their existence at sixteen years, rather than at sixteen weeks.

gestion would certainly make a far better deterrent to sneaking out at night than grounding.

Whenever a human being is entitled to decide whether another human being actually IS human, you know you're on the same path trodden by all the ethnic cleansers of history. Why do we even discuss whether a pre-born baby is human? We have to, because lodged in the conscience of every human being that reaches the age of inductive and/or deductive reasoning is the knowledge that to destroy one of your own is wrong. As the Nazis (the easy go-to guys when you want to describe the worst of humanity), and anyone else into this racial purity nonsense knew, you must always dehumanize a human before you are allowed to kill one.

Let me give you an example of how perception changes reality. A man comes home from work after an exceptionally hard day. He's tired and frustrated and simply wants to go home and relax. When he arrives, he finds the house dark save for two candles burning romantically on the table. The best china and silverware are laid out, and a wonderful smell emanates from the kitchen.

He goes to his room, where he quickly showers and puts on his robe and slippers. When he arrives in the dining room, his wife is waiting for him, looking beautiful and radiant. As he sits down to an amazing gourmet meal and finishes an intoxicating glass of his favorite merlot, his wife lovingly stares at him across the table and with moist eyes and a warm heart says simply, "Honey . . . we're having a baby."

Any couple who has experienced this miracle knows that the joy is literally indescribable.

Now, it's important to note that when a woman first finds out she's pregnant, she could conceivably (no pun intended) be only four to six weeks along. She isn't having the baby now and won't for quite a while. The baby is only beginning its life cycle, and it will be a long time before it PHYSICALLY LOOKS human. But as far as this couple is concerned, it's time to paint the nursery and call their parents, because in their minds they are having a baby!

I want to take this same scenario and give it a different twist. In this scene, the husband comes home to find the house pretty much the way he left it that morning. He finds his wife resting in the living room, oblivious to his arrival. She finally notices him and lets him know his dinner is in the microwave, all he has to do is push START. He eats alone at the dining room table, reading the paper, then gives her a kiss good night, as he's retiring early. She continues to watch TV and takes some aspirin for the dull ache she feels from the "procedure" she had that morning.

Same woman, same man. Only this woman has just had an abortion. What's the difference? In the first scenario, the child was wanted; in the second, it wasn't. But the child didn't become inhuman the moment it was no longer desired. The baby in the first scenario was still a baby in the second; you'll never hear anyone who desires a child EVER refer to him or her as tissue or a zygote or anything other than their baby and a potential tax write-off. They give it significance because it's significant to them. That's why you never hear an aborted child referred to as a baby. It's an "operation" or a "procedure," and it's worded strategically to dehumanize the action, allowing the conscience to feel validated.

Death is, simply, the proof of the wrongness of abortion. When a woman is pregnant, that zygote, left to its own devices,

You'll never hear anyone who desires a child EVER refer to him or her as tissue or a zygote or anything other than their baby and a potential tax write-off.

usually evolves into a fully biologically developed human. When this natural process is interrupted, the human dies.

We know that fully developed humans are dead when their heart, lungs, and brain cease to function. That is the end of life. So it stands to reason that if that is the end of life, then the beginning of life must occur when this human's development is kicked into motion. At conception. At that point everything needed to create another of God's creatures is in place, and all we have to do is leave it alone and allow it to develop at its own uninterrupted pace.

Now granted, in the beginning, it is very, very small. Which is one of the reasons that some scientists posit that it's OK to destroy. Since it doesn't look like us YET, and doesn't breathe on its own YET, and doesn't reason within itself YET, it isn't worthy of protection. No matter if you are black or white, born to

No matter if you are black or white, born to rich parents or poor, turn out gay or straight, we all, at one time, held the minority status of being really small.

rich parents or poor, turn out gay or straight, we all, at one time, held the minority status of being really small. (Welcome to MY world!)

Perception, once again, is the key here, as the liberal ideologue ignores the real issue that a human being who happens to be "different" (even microscopic) from the rest of us deserves to be treated with respect and dignity, which is ironically the same argument they use to champion every other fringe lifestyle they believe deserves protection. I think it's telling that the only people who are capable of even discussing whether abortion is legitimate are people who weren't aborted.

But enough of this cheeriness, let's find something heavy to talk about.

☆ 18 ☆

Wishing I'd Win the Lottery in Vegas

Part of the fun of living in America is the idea that someday you may strike it rich. This idea is so deeply ingrained in our society that even liberals don't question the premise.

Take Las Vegas, for instance. Vegas is one of the fastest growing cities in the United States, and it got that way by instigating that tried-and-true American tradition of . . . ripping you off. I'm surprised there hasn't been a book written about this unique business formula: "You give us a thousand dollars, we'll give you . . . NOTHING! If that's not enough, after two hours, we'll double it! GUARANTEED." Americans have fallen for get-rich-quick schemes since the first pilgrim stepped foot on this continent. Of course, then the second pilgrim jumped out of the boat onto this great land, picked up a rock, claimed it as the original, and sold tickets.

We Americans today like to think we're more sophisticated than our pilgrim forebears. Today, if you visit this fake original rock, you'll see it comes with an informative video presentation

Americans have fallen for get-rich-quick schemes since the first pilgrim stepped foot on this continent.

to lend credence to the scam . . . AND you can purchase a T-shirt on the way out! The truth is, we're not any more sophisticated than the pilgrims when it comes to that age-old human tendency known as curiosity. It's our natural childlike desire for things too good to be true to *be* true that brings something like . . . the wishing well to light.

The "wishing well" had to have been created by the same people who brought us Vegas, that liberal something-for-nothing concept they use so well to manipulate voters, because it offers the exact same results. Make a wish, we'll take your money, and we'll give you . . . nothing. OK, maybe that's a bit harsh. Give us your money and we'll give you . . . false hope in return! What's even more amazing to me than the fact that the wishing well exists at all is the fact that people—and not just little kids, but full-grown adults—fall for it, again and again. Show me a fountain, a well, a wading pool, or any small collection of water that happens to be in a public place, and I'll show you a thousand dollars worth of change.

It seems to me that one of the criteria for investing money in a well that grants wishes is, eventually, you actually get a wish granted. Of course, not only does this never happen, but because of the liberal guilt machine that has taught parents that if they deny their children something, then they could be arrested, parents joyfully pass this tradition on to their kids. Children *must* come out of this experience with a clearer view of economic issues: "OK, you won't give me money for gum at the checkout line in the grocery store because I 'don't need it,' but you're happy to dig out every last bit of change from the bottom of your purse so I can toss it into a fountain!"

But lest you think I'm a wishing-well naysayer, I'm willing to take the concept a bit further than anyone in the history of wishing wells ever has before. In fact, I recently discovered when I moved into my new house that my front yard isn't just an ordinary yard . . . it's a *wishing yard*. Isn't that wonderful? My kids are thrilled. All you have to do is drive past my house and throw cash onto the lawn. You don't even have to stop, just toss the cash (preferably stacks of bills, or gold coins if you don't have a rubber band) and go home and *wish real hard* for anything you want. Really, anything.

> My front yard is a *wishing yard*. Drive past my house and throw cash onto the lawn. Wish real hard for what you want.

If after seven days your wish hasn't come true, it only proves that you didn't want it badly enough. And that's too bad. But you can keep trying! Drive on by, throw some cash onto my lawn, and wish, wish some more. You never know what good could come of believing in fairy tales.

The next best thing to a wishing well is a lottery ticket. Look at the billions of dollars spent every year on lottery tickets by people who can't afford them but are willing to gamble what little they have in the hopes of striking it rich. Now, we all know the possibility of hitting the lottery is astronomically low, but that doesn't stop your average American from trying, as they believe getting rich is their birthright. And true to that pipe dream, the lottery odds are always framed in a statistical way to showcase your likelihood of winning it, which for reasons that are unclear to me, directly correspond with your likelihood of being killed in a natural disaster.

"This week's jackpot is five hundred million dollars! Get out there and buy those tickets!" Then, in a low voice, "Statistically, you have the same chance of hitting this lottery as [insert fatal catastrophe here]." One of the cruelest of ironies when it comes to this "lottery or killed" scenario is to consider all the natural disasters that actually do kill people each year. The one time in your life you beat the odds . . . and you're DEAD!

So I guess the moral of the story is, if you ever get hit by lightning, immediately buy a lottery ticket. But if you ever hit the lottery, take some of your winnings and go invest in some rubber shoes.

☆ 19 ☆

Why Baseball Is Conservative America's Favorite Sport

I grew up playing and watching baseball, and will go to my grave as a Dodger fan. Baseball, of course, is the all-American game and a decidedly conservative game, which is why it has endured, whereas the liberal-minded pastimes such as marathon dancing and underwater pogo-stick races have thankfully fallen by the wayside.

What makes baseball conservative America's favorite sport? Let me count the ways. The equipment used in baseball, for example, is concise and reasonable. Baseball has one bat that is used for hitting, bunting, and smashing water coolers. There is one glove for an infielder, one for an outfielder, one for a first baseman, and one for a catcher, as opposed to golf, which is far more complicated than it needs to be, in part because each player is forced to own lots of different clubs because NONE of them works properly. You constantly have to try a different one on every shot with the hope of finding the right club.

> In golf, each player is forced to own lots of different clubs because NONE of them works properly.

Golf started out as a fun, leisurely, conservative-minded game, but for some reason, over time, somebody got ahold of it and completely went off the deep end by overcomplicating it. I can't prove it was a liberal who screwed it up, but anytime something simple that's fun and makes sense suddenly becomes convoluted with red tape and bureaucracy, well, you can draw your own conclusions.

The first thing you are supposed to do in golf is drive the ball down the fairway. The "way" is "fair" because it's straight and full of plenty of space, nothing fairer than that. Instead, you will find these alleged golfers complicating things by trying to hit the ball with a club that couldn't possibly be considered appropriate for the task. What happened to driving the ball? Look, conservatives even provided the cart! Instead, the liberal interpreted "driving" to mean "hitting" but considered "hitting" a word that would send the wrong message to our children. But look what I'm left with: a thin-shafted stick with a bulbous metal head attached to it, and that's what I'm supposed to hit the two-inch ball with. Instead of having one bat that's shaped the same so everyone has to adapt to the same equipment, the liberal decided it was an unfair advantage to expect such diligence, since the monopoly on diligence and hard work is squarely in the conservative camp, so they made up a whole variety of different-shaped club heads so we could choose which one to screw up with. Of course, the ever-entrepreneurial conservative went ahead and made a big business out of manufacturing these clubs, which is the only upside.

Once you've driven the ball quite a ways down the fairway, you will find these golfers trying to hit it again with a long iron. (None of the irons, by the way, are even made of iron; instead, they are graphite and steel and any host of non-iron, space-age material.) The closer you get to the hole, the more hungry you become, as you're told to "chip it" from here. Chips, pretzels, anything snacklike would go well with the drink that your cart is carrying in its cup holder. You're given food and drink to carry with you along the way, in case the game starts to become too demanding (only a liberal would come up with that) and, of course, my people are right there with the concessions to provide more jobs and a higher GNP.

So you drive all the way down the fairway, eat and drink at every hole, and then, after smacking the ball with all you got, you finally get to the green, where you're expected to "putt" the ball. The liberal, of course, must have figured this is the only time in the game where everyone will be together (I know, since I spend most of my time in the woods) so they want you to "putt" the ball softly at the end so no one gets hurt (plus, they don't want to promote violence). Leave it to a liberal bureaucrat to invent a word by adding an extra "t" to "put." After all I've gone through to get here, I should simply be able to pick the ball up and "put" it in the cup, call it a day, and go home.

It's because of these ridiculous, overly complicated requirements that you see far fewer fans watching a golf game than a baseball game. Only golf punishes its spectators by charging them to walk the length of the course in a socialist type of "the players are no better than us" mentality. So, basically, I stink at golf, and I like to think it's the liberals' fault.

> Only golf punishes its spectators by charging them to walk the length of the course.

Then, there's football. Just to set the record straight, since I'm not a fan of being beaten up, I want to make it clear that I am not anti-football. Football is a good game, a really, really, good game, BUT baseball is a great game. Baseball was the first American game, and that fact alone makes it the greatest. First is always best. McDonald's was the first of the fast-food franchises, and by far the most successful. Their hamburgers are still horrible, but they are selling them in Red Square in China, which in and of itself is a testimony to the power of first. But the most obvious distinction between the sophisticated baseball fan and the crude rudimentary football fan becomes strikingly apparent when you compare their rooting techniques, and is a wonderful illustration of the conservative/liberal approaches to life. Conservatives *use* their minds, liberals *lose* theirs.

The first and obvious upside to baseball is that it's played in the summer. Because it is a summertime, pastoral game, baseball invokes times of childhood and innocence and also encourages the freedom to respond to the weather in a truly summerlike fashion. Baseball fans can take off their shirts because it's July and it's hot. Football fans trying to mimic their baseball counterparts take off their shirts, too, but since it's, say, Pittsburgh in

December, they come across not so much as fans but more along the lines of the mentally ill who are unaware it's forty below. There is a not-so-subtle difference between removing your shirt in the summer because that's always been a summer tradition and taking off your shirt AND jacket in the winter to show solidarity with your team, who never shows up to visit when you end up in intensive care for hypothermia. Baseball fans wear their favorite team's hat in public in tribute to their allegiance and respect, but you never see football fans wearing their favorite team's *helmet* in public. Sure, they wear their oversize jerseys, but rarely will they include the shoulder pads, which, once again, shows their fair-weather support and comes straight out of the liberal handbook for how not to make a commitment.

A baseball hat can be worn as a stylish accessory even when you are dressed up, whereas the football duffel bag sadly has not caught on as the "it" purse of the fall season. In fact, some smart conservative came up with the idea of creating baseball hats with football logos because even the football aficionado had to concede that a hat with a brim is more stylish and practical than a hat with a chinstrap and a face mask.

A baseball hat can be worn as a stylish accessory even when you are dressed up, whereas the football duffel bag sadly has not caught on as the "it" purse of the fall season.

Baseball fans are so respected by team owners that if a ball used in the game ends up in their area, they are allowed to keep it, illustrating the conservative capitalist mind that celebrates the fact that if you're willing to catch a line drive with your bare hands, you are rewarded for your entrepreneurial ingenuity and grit. A football that is kicked or otherwise ends up in the stands has to be given back because the coaches only had the foresight to bring *one,* and besides, we don't want to hurt the feelings of the fans who didn't get one. Baseball has a seventh inning stretch where they encourage circulation at both ends of the inning, so you can pay tribute to the team you are supporting. Even when you're in the opposing team's stadium, you stand proud, willing to take the gibes and insults thrown your way because you're an American and have the right to disagree even in the face of your dissenters. Football, on the other hand, has a halftime show where they have to feature entertainment in order to keep people interested and to make sure everyone feels like they're getting their money's worth.

Baseball players, like their fellow conservatives, must be smarter than football players, as they must be able to defy physics. After hitting the ball (a sphere traveling 90 m.p.h.) with a bat (which is just a fancy word for wooden club), baseball players are able to "round" the bases that are in the shape of a diamond! Football players had to be given a field that only goes in one direction—straight. They even had to create out-of-bounds sidelines to constantly reinforce and remind them which way to go! Baseball counts as its fans George Will, Rudy Giuliani, and Stephen King. Football attracts guys who are still wrestling with the possibility of literacy. A baseball game doesn't end until it's over. One of the game's sages even said so. There are no ties in baseball because it's a game and, as such, someone's going to lose, so get over it! Extra innings are added until the war is over, even if it carries over into the next day, reminiscent of the battles Americans have fought over the years. We never gave up until the enemy surrendered or was annihilated, and that was America!

A baseball game doesn't end until it's over. Football had to make time limits, since they don't want to push anybody too hard. What would the union say?

Football had to make time limits so the players and coaches would understand how much time should be needed to complete the game. Time limits, of course, mean that we don't want to push anybody too hard or too unreasonably—what would the union say if they were expected to work and actually earn their multimillion-dollar keep! Something called "sudden death" was created, which basically amounts to overtime, the liberal version of "let's get this over with and go home ASAP." Baseball also has no salary cap, which coincides with the notion that if you own a team and are willing to spend $5 million on a third-string catcher, don't come crying to me if you lose money. Football instituted the cap since liberals always believe they know how to spend your money better than the guy who owns the team.

Football even had to allow for "time-outs" so they could regroup and catch their breath instead of improvising on the fly, like true entrepreneurs. Baseball would proudly display its American ideal of world dominance by calling its biggest game the World Series even before the rest of the world learned to play. Our conviction that no one else would ever play it as well as we would has proved to be true after all these years. Football called its big game the Super Bowl, based on the size of its fans' nachos containers.

Baseball calls its biggest game the World Series. Football's Super Bowl came from the size of its fans' nachos container.

Baseball is also the all-American sport in its inclusiveness, and not just nationalities but body types. Some of baseballs greatest stars were fat. Babe Ruth was known for his gargantuan appetite, and still he managed to be one of the greatest players of all time. Short guys like Freddie Patek and Pee Wee Reese were able to compete right alongside the sickeningly tall.

In baseball, Hispanics pitch to blacks as Europeans and left-ies all work together in harmony with seventy-year-old managers running the team, since baseball treasures the old and wise. (Heck, baseball's even had two guys with ONE ARM make the team.) That's America, and that's why baseball is America's perfect conservative sport.

Not to mention, no putting.

☆ 20 ☆

God, According to the Atheist

No concept in this country is more likely to create divisiveness, anger, and vitriol among human beings than the concept of a loving God.

What's interesting about God in the liberal new-world order is that you are actually allowed to believe in him, as long as you don't call him a him. God in liberal la-la land is always referred to in the form of bland spirituality ("Yes, I believe in *something,* I'm a very spiritual person") or, worse, in a woo-woo California way (which means any mention of the universe, the life force. This basically means that any belief you have about God, or no God, is equally OK).

Relativism is an absolute must in the spiritual world of liberal ideology because claiming any absolute truth about God might interfere with the liberal's "spiritual" experimentation, which always results in the amazing discovery that he, the liberal himself, is God. But even liberals can't escape the fact that since the beginning of recorded human history, we've all been on a continual search for God. Carl Sagan was absolutely convinced that there was intelligent life somewhere in the universe. Now, as a conservative Christian living in Middle America, I have no problem letting scientists explore the universe searching for E.T., but I don't need confirmation that there's a God out there, especially when such exploration comes out of my tax dollars!

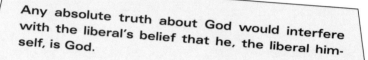

Any absolute truth about God would interfere with the liberal's belief that he, the liberal himself, is God.

Billions of bucks are spent on satellite devices that probe the outer reaches of the galaxy searching for a group of beings that are always (according to the movies) more intelligent than us, more peaceful, and, of course, more philanthropic in their willingness to share their wisdom and technology. After all, as Americans, we stand to learn a lot from . . . aliens.

As Americans, we stand to learn a lot from aliens.

What's most fascinating about this philosophy that there is intelligent life that has never been seen but is just waiting for us to be nicer to each other so "it" can come to Earth and redeem us is that the same definition applies to the Judeo-Christian God! It's amazing that such a theory is accepted as plausible when it comes to us in the name of "science." But when the liberal pseudo-intellectual is reminded that God is someone we have never seen, lives somewhere we have never found, is always nicer to us than we are to ourselves, and seems to be waiting for us to be good to each other so he can come down and redeem us, THIS is instantly categorized as "myth" and dismissed as superstitious nonsense. So, if you want to be taken seriously as an intellectual in this country, it's obvious you must lean on the rational side of the space aliens in their flying saucers.

One of the classic falsehoods you can expect to hear about God and religion is that more people have been killed in the name of religion than anything else. So, if I were to use logic (which proves right there I'm not a liberal), I would venture that if theism has caused the most harm to society, then atheism must have brought about the greatest good. Gee, are there any examples from human history in which a people were ruled by atheism? Oh yeah, that wonderfully human rights–driven system known as . . . drum roll, please . . . COMMUNISM. Yes, folks, you heard it from the liberals first: If you want to clean up your community, get yourself a Stalin! Now, let's not shortchange the atheist—there's also Pol Pot, Khrushchev, Mao Tsetung, Kim Jong Il, and that old life-lovin' softy, Castro!

Let's examine for a moment these two belief systems. First, since in America, the hatred and bigotry toward religion is more accurately defined as hatred toward Christianity, let's start there. Being a Christian, I know that my religion teaches me to love others and not to kill—which, in the biblical context, means murder. Yes, there have been deaths caused in the name of Christianity, but "in the name of" is the operative phrase. It was the *misuse* of the religion that caused death, not the belief system itself. We certainly don't condemn the value of a car or a plane just because some idiot uses this particular transportation vehicle as a killing machine! (Plus, liberals can rejoice in the knowledge that if people continue to be killed by cars, we could always ban them as "unsafe.")

If you add up all the deaths caused by religion, be it the Crusades, the Salem witch trials, Islamic terrorism, Protestant/ Catholic clashes, or the Spanish Inquisition, we might be talking about 50 to 100 million people over a few thousand years. *Not* to diminish those lives, but in looking at the sheer numbers, which the liberal atheist would urge us to do, we'd have to compare our tally to the estimated 200 million lives that have been wasted since the early nineteen hundreds at the hands of the atheists in communist countries.

You gotta hand it to them. They broke the religious abusers' record in less than a hundred years! Talk about a quick study! Those atheists, when they want to get things done, they don't mess around.

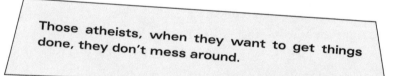

Those atheists, when they want to get things done, they don't mess around.

Now, in calculating deaths caused by religion, I failed to mention the lives saved by Christianity. Realizing that no other culture considered taking care of those outside its immediate family as its responsibility, Jesus spoke of the good Samaritan, which led to the Christian idea of hospitality, that later became known as hospitals. Let us also not forget that it was people driven by their religious beliefs who stopped the slave trade, protected children, and gave rights to women and to peoples of different religions. Not counting the millions saved from alcoholism because of Alcoholics Anonymous and the Salvation Army, as well as missionaries who have drilled freshwater wells in Africa, brought education and sanitation to third-world countries, and are at the forefront in the battle against AIDS in Africa, this much-despised Christianity has by far saved more lives than were killed and gave hope to those the atheists ignored.

Where I come from—and I mean Middle America as much as I mean as a follower of Christ—being good to others is not just a human belief, it's a religious belief. So when an atheist tells you he's moral, just politely point out that he's borrowing from religion to even make a moral claim, because in the world he believes in, where humans are an accident, morals not only don't exist, they are irrelevant. Why? Because if a culture alone decides what's moral, then a standard isn't *actually* a moral standard at all. It's a cultural standard that changes when the culture tires of it.

> Where I come from, being good to others is not just a human belief, it's a religious belief.

That's why we never can hide from the God debate. It seems to be an essential part of our nature. Believer or not, humans naturally gravitate toward the idea of an afterlife, since the life we have now is way too short, often tedious, and riddled with bloating and gas.

☆ **21** ☆

Snoopy in Drag at the Macy's Thanksgiving Day Parade

I saw my first gay pride parade in San Francisco, which may not be the best way for a Middle American man like me to ease into this unorthodox experience. Anyone who has ever seen a gay pride parade knows pretty quickly that what passes for appropriate costuming for a gay parade is completely different from that of a straight one. When the parade was first created, it was, I believe, a statement made by a group of Americans celebrating their sexual preference as it differed from that of the mainstream. (Though I am someone who enjoys heterosexual sex [with my wife], I must admit, for some reason, this preference never struck me as something that warranted a marching band and a grand marshal.) I think where the gay parade has gone astray is that it now seems designed to convince the 99 percent of America that isn't gay that they are just like us.

OK, if that is their mission, then may I play straight eye for the queer guy for a second and offer a bit of advice regarding their presentation? TONE IT DOWN a bit. You could start by

PUTTING ON SOME PANTS! It's tough enough for me to follow the plotline when the guy's objective is to look like a woman, and the woman's main objective is to look like a man. Then, when you least expect it, you get a group of guys *who look like guys* appearing to have just walked out of a locker room, wearing everything for the big game *except* their uniforms. So either this is some kind of homage to "kabuki theater meets Milton Berle" that I'm too square to fully grasp or it's setting me up so when the guys in athletic supporters come dancing down the street I'll cry out, "Finally, a restore to order."

> Is this some kind of homage to "kabuki theater meets Milton Berle" that I'm too square to grasp?

I hope we don't see this trend cropping up in other parades, by the way. Could you imagine if the Macy's Thanksgiving Day parade looked like that? Try explaining that to your kids, because I just don't think the country is quite ready for the three-hundred-foot Garfield balloon wearing a leather jockstrap! Or Superman in a boa and stiletto heels wielding a whip. (No wonder they call him *Super*man.) What interesting conversations that would make with the children: "Look, Mommy, Snoopy's in drag!" "Yes honey, doesn't he look . . . umm . . . proud?"

Now, before any of the logically impaired liberals out there accuse me of gay bashing, let me explain something. If you go around in public during a parade in nothing but a jockstrap and think that if someone comments on it it's "bashing," then you are on your way to being inducted into the moron hall of fame.

Liberals seem to want a world where nothing is outrageous or, and more important, inappropriate, and by redefining the argument to making the *commentator* bad just by bringing it up, they are creating a world where censorship in reverse rules the day. As a democratic republic, we all have the right to try and get society to accept us, no matter what package that comes in. If enough do, YOU WIN, that's democracy! But when that right is manipulated into a liberal-minded brand of anti-Christian bashing, we're going to fight for our own rights to have a clear Christian conviction.

I knew things were really getting strange when the word "homophobia" began to hit the streets. Being accused of being homophobic doesn't make sense because, first of all, "homophobia" is not a real word. If you look at the root of the word, you'd be led to believe that if you disagree with ANY part of the homosexual point of view, you have a mental disorder. That's what a phobia is! If disagreeing with a homosexual's belief amounts to homophobia, then by the laws of logic, those who disagree with me are suffering from heterophobia! Welcome to the club.

I miss the old days when homosexuals knew they were different from most of society and fought for THAT right. It seems to me if I were gay, the right to be left alone no matter how different I was would make for an even more noble fight than mainstream acceptance. And yet, the liberal believes that the world is a better place if we pretend that no matter how different people actually are, if we *say* we're the same, then all is well. As conservatives, we actually believe *in an even more liberal world* that allows our differences to be left where they are, and lets people decide how they are going to deal with it in society. This makes for an even freer way of living as well since it doesn't demand conformity to the latest special-interest group. The risk of living in a democracy is that once in a while you're not going to get the consensus no matter how magnanimous you believe your struggle.

One of the biggest hypocrisies with the liberal mind is that the only standard they will accept is the one that doesn't allow immutable standards. Look, if we have reached a point in society where expecting pants to be worn by parade members is too much to ask, then don't come crying to me when the elderly nudist pride parade comes marching to a town near you. Trust me, you'll be BEGGING for underpants.

Hillary Clinton's Bible Lesson

Since many of my closest family members are gay, I obviously want them to be happy and to be able to live free of violence and malicious attacks. But that doesn't mean I should be denied the right to believe what I believe, especially when it comes to marriage. I come from a divorced family, as does my wife, and I can speak from firsthand experience when I say there is no better formula for a child's upbringing than the one that's been in place since the beginning of human history: one dad and one mom, committed in marriage, staying together, till death do them part.

I know there are other family scenarios that exist today, but I still believe in the tried-and-true, one of each gender. Not two dads, whether that comes in the form of two gay men OR a real dad and a stepdad. Not two moms, not a single mom by choice, just your basic, run-of-the-mill one of each.

To be honest, I don't even understand the concept of gay marriage. Let me get this straight: Guys want to marry guys?

COWARDS! Where's the challenge? Part of what makes marriage so great is when a male and female learn to live together twenty-four hours a day without one or the other slitting their wrists. I think it would be EASY to be married to a guy! None of the myriad problems that arise in a normal marriage (THAT'S RIGHT, NORMAL, I'm not going to argue semantics with those who run from the truth) would ever play out in a same-gender marriage. I would never have to say, "Hon, where is the shirt I was wearing yesterday?" because I would *know* where it was. It would still be in the corner where I tossed it the night before because, both of us being guys, *neither of us* would have picked it up!

I don't even understand the concept of gay marriage. Guys want to marry guys? Where's the challenge?

But I agree: This issue must be addressed in a logical and respectful way as long as we acknowledge that sometimes what we want is more than what society must give us. The other day I saw a gay-marriage advocate wearing a T-shirt that read, "Marriage is a human right, not a heterosexual privilege." Actually, my friend, a heterosexual privilege is EXACTLY what marriage is. There are many privileges in society that are confined to a specific group. Like the privilege to vote at eighteen, not seventeen and a half. Like the privilege to drive a car, not the right to. Like the privilege to become president of the United States only if you were born here, not the right to aspire to it, though

Arnold seems to be exploring the loopholes in that dilemma. The conservative mind absolutely owes a real hard look at making sure compassion is not neutralized for the sake of a law. Not in the carte blanche access to all things hetero, but certainly the right to have anyone you want at your hospital sickbed, or the right to leave your worldly goods to whomever you choose.

Hillary Clinton (like I could write a conservative book and not have that name pop up eventually), speaking at Tufts University in Massachusetts, made this comment: "Liberals need to use the BIBLE to argue the moral issue of poverty just like the conservatives used it to argue against gay marriage." Clearly, the desire of the American people to keep marriage as is and as it has been for thousands of years was passed overwhelmingly in the 2004 elections. But what the liberal mind must grasp is the fact that this desire crossed all gender, race, and political lines. The *majority* of blacks, women, evangelicals, Kerry supporters, and Oregon residents (including the elderly that hadn't yet killed themselves) all voted AGAINST gay marriage! It was apparently not a "Christian Right" issue, nor was it the decisive issue that helped Bush win the presidency.

> The *majority* of blacks, women, evangelicals, Kerry supporters, and Oregon residents all voted AGAINST gay marriage!

The proof is in the fact that there were gay-marriage referendums in eleven states, yet in those states President Bush increased his vote by less than in the thirty-nine states that *had no such referendum.* But just like the Matthew Shepard case, in which his killers admitted that he was robbed for drugs but the fact that he was gay was used to exploit his death to fuel the antigay hate-crime fire, nothing is more dishonorable than to lie in order to make an alleged "moral" point.

But back to Hillary's Bible lesson. I can say, unequivocally, that if liberals begin to use the Bible as a tool to exploit their agenda, in trying to garner votes, they are in for an even longer dry spell politically than they could ever imagine. Liberals see the Bible as something that brings authority to their view of an issue, which sounds opportunistic because it is. Conservatives cite the Bible as the ultimate authority on all things that are true because that's how we live our lives. The Bible informs how we think *every day,* not just every four years. While we believe our belief system is "true," based on the image the Founding Fathers had for this great country, the liberal's belief system is simply based on their opinion. And that's why the liberal-minded ships constantly end up on the rocks. You can't pick and choose the morals that work for you from the Bible. It's the greatest book ever published for a reason, and it's not up for a revision!

> You can't pick and choose the morals that work for you from the Bible. It's the greatest book ever published for a reason, and it's not up for a revision!

Now, I am an open-minded conservative, so if Hillary has something to teach me from the Bible, I'm willing to listen. She definitely has experience when it comes to forgiveness. As for all of my gay friends and family, I will always love and respect you for what I have learned from you. We will not always see eye to eye, but you know you can count on me if you need me, and I know I can count on you if I need you as well. If for no other reason than to be my interpreter at your parades.

☆ 23 ☆

How TV Commercials Build Character

One of the problems with the liberalization of America is that it has deprived our kids of the ability to think for themselves, to exercise their minds, and to get ripped off honorably, the way we used to. Think about the commercials we had in the seventies, back in the days before some liberal senator created some kind of liberal commission that forced advertisers to include disclaimers. The old commercials did us all a public service by preparing us to be discerning consumers!

Remember the slogan, "Four out of five dentists recommend sugarless gum for their patients who chew gum"? At first glance, "for their patients who chew gum" might strike you as its own kind of qualifier. But think about "four out of five." That means, somewhere in America, there was a dentist who was not completely convinced that sugar was bad for your teeth! Or maybe, just maybe, he had an ulterior motive? Maybe, in the spirit of old-fashioned American entrepreneurship, this one

> One of the problems with the liberalization of America is that it has deprived our kids of the opportunity to get ripped off honorably, the way we used to.

holdout thought about his three kids in college and decided it was in his interest to ensure repeat customers. So his visits always came with the recommendation to chew as much sugar*ful* gum as you could get your hands on! "Nah, the research proves nothing. Isn't the sugared gum so much tastier? Chew as much as possible! And hey, if you run out of gum . . . suck on some sugar packets! Wash it down with Mountain Dew!"

I HAD this dentist! He was the guy who gave you a sucker after cleaning your teeth.

We need more commercials today that teach kids to be street-smart. And nothing prepares your character for the real world like the old car commercials. I miss USED CARS! That's right, back in the day when we were honest enough to call them "used." Today, they're referred to as "pre-owned" cars, to which I respond, if you're going to insult my intelligence, why stop there? Why not "formerly loved" cars or "driven now and again" cars? This is just another example of the dumbing down of America, courtesy of the liberal ideologue who felt that calling cars "used" would hurt their feelings. How stupid do they think the public is? "Yeah, we are selling pre-owned cars, sure somebody else *owned* the car, but they . . . didn't . . . uhh . . . *use* it!"

Why do you think kids nowadays are constantly getting tat-

Today, *used* cars are referred to as "pre-owned." Why stop there? Why not "formerly loved" or "driven now and again" cars?

toos and piercing their body with jewelry? They have developed a self-loathing and internal angst brought on by not learning the art of defending themselves. They feel vulnerable and useless, and so they have to compensate by altering their bodies to look like what we used to call "graffiti." I believe even *that* word has been replaced with the word . . . "art"?

Kids need to be able to practice defending themselves from other tribes that may try to invade the village, so to speak. So, they wear the modern war paint (tattoos) to give themselves and those around them the illusion that they are strong and self-reliant. Why they think their Tweety Bird tattoo is supposed to frighten us into thinking they're dangerous proves just how out of touch with reality they have become.

What drives me especially crazy about kids who pierce themselves is that piercing always comes with that teenage attitude that is somehow supposed to impress adults who are twice their age and are not easily impressed. They think they are actually doing something on the edge, something incredibly courageous, by piercing their tongue. Sorry, kids, but if the most radical thing you can come up with is an earring in your tongue, you just wasted fifty bucks and three weeks' worth of a self-imposed speech impediment.

Why not come home with two adult-size Ubangi lip plates lodged in your mouth! THAT would be impressive coming home from the mall. ("Mom, Dad, look what I did!") THAT would be edgy.

Or, you really want to do something that will blow your parents' minds?

Get a job.

The liberal-minded environment that has influenced this new millennium has left our kids unable to fend for themselves and unaware of what they don't know. As a result, we've ended up with children who are restless, insecure, have never known boundaries, and are trapped in some kind of post-hippie mentality that never learned a thing from the obvious destruction of character that evolved out of what I'd consider the single most immature and cowardly phrase ever to come out of the sixties: "If it feels good, do it."

Liberals live by the motto, "Nothing matters but me." Humans, particularly humans just like themselves, are, in their minds, gods. The fact that humans are flawed, the fact that we have always had war, killing, destruction, hate, violence, selfishness, and oppression, still does not register with their utopian vision that if we simply pretend to be nice, somehow we actually are.

The truth is, there's not a lot that liberals have to complain about. They're the ones who championed no restrictions on television. Since every other commercial on TV is selling food, our kids now have the choice to be fat. Liberals created a new type of Barbie doll called "Bratz" that teaches little girls how to dress provocatively—at the age of six. Liberals paved the way for TV commercials featuring condoms and erectile dysfunction, so luckily we now have the choice (and the assistance) to enjoy meaningless sex.

Seems to me, the liberal utopia of a freer, more immoral society is fast becoming a reality. Dang. All I wanted were lawn darts.

☆ 24 ☆

Why I'd Rather Be Fat Than Short

I love when people (especially liberals) say, "Since I'm a woman/man/Jew/Muslim/fat person/short person, *I can say this*." This qualifier usually comes before a comment that would be misconstrued as offensive by anyone not in that select group, but because the speaker is *also* a woman/man/Jew/Muslim/fat person/short person, they feel they have license to say anything they want about someone in their tribe without fear of recrimination from the PC word police.

That just smells like a double standard to me. Since conservatives seek (and speak) the truth without the qualifiers, I feel safe in sharing the fact that I am short.

I measure in at an intimidating five-foot-six, which by any account is below average unless your data includes pygmies. Notice in a very unliberal fashion I used the term "below average" (and the term "pygmies"), meaning I am abnormal. So what?

If you tell me I'm short, I *can't* be offended, whether you yourself are five feet or seven feet, because *it's true*. And yet,

I measure in at an intimidating five-foot-six, which by any account is below average unless your data includes pygmies.

short people are some of the most maligned in society. Calling someone "a small man" is not a compliment, nor is the term "small-minded." Short people are assumed to have an attitude about their diminutive size, called the Napoleon complex, where through achievement or arrogance or the size of our desk we appear to be overcompensating for being short. Maybe we're overcompensating for being overlooked?

Short people have to earn every speck of respect they can garner. Tall people don't have this problem. They are just assumed to be athletic, for example. Every tall person has heard, at some point in their lives, "You're tall, do you play basketball?" This is assumed to be a compliment, even if this tall person is not athletic at all. What do they say to the short guy? "You're short, uhh, are you a jockey?" In baseball, we have the shortstop; he doesn't even get his own base! "OK, guys, first base, you go to second, third for you and, oh yeah, short guy, when the ball comes to you . . . just stop it!"

The truth is, I'd much rather be fat than short. At least fat people get to be jolly. Everything about fat comes with a positive spin, in comparison to being short. Fat people get to be Santa; short people get to be elves. Fat implies abundance; short, a lacking. A fat wallet is a good thing, not to mention a fat paycheck to fill it, in comparison to "shortage" (not enough) and "short-changed" (ripped off!).

Fat people get to be Santa; short people get to be elves.

Back in medieval times, the fat girls were the babes! Being fat proved your upper-class status in society, since you were obviously eating well and, even more obviously, not exercising much. The great artists of their time painted the fat girl posed on a chaise . . . naked . . . eating! THAT is a healthy body image! They were round and voluptuous, which was worshipped, not tan and thin, which was avoided because it meant you were a laborer, low class, looked down upon, and expected to supply the fat girls with something to eat.

Food was hard to come by in those days, so the best food was stored on the highest shelves to avoid rats and mildew, which also meant the short people (my ancestors) couldn't reach it. (Historical note: Ladders were too expensive for peasants to afford; the best we could come up with was sitting or standing on each other's shoulders, which I believe is how short people invented circus tumbling routines.)

Now, the liberal would likely take issue with the fact that I'm neither a fat girl myself nor am I using the liberal-approved synonyms for "fat," such as "full-figured," "large," "plus-sized," or "big-boned." In their twisted logic to make everyone feel good, liberals end up stigmatizing the very same people they're trying to protect.

I say fat is fat, and those among us should be given the dignity of being (and saying) exactly who and what they are. Liberals try to fix society's ills, not by instituting any real change but by using different words so it *sounds* like we are making progress. Our country isn't better because we can't say a fat person is fat, our country is better when fat isn't considered less valuable than thin.

We should thank God daily that we live in a country where we enjoy an abundance that gives us the *option* of getting fat. In fact, maybe we should motivate all justice-seeking conservatives to try to assist other countries in fattening up their people! Remember that wise old saying, "Inside every fat person there's a thin person saying, 'I'm still hungry!'" Or, in my case, inside every tall person there's a short person saying: "Hey, buddy, can you press floor eighty-seven, I can't reach!"

☆ 25 ☆

You Say "Little Person," I Say "Midget"

Jesus said the truth will set you free, which, by implication, must mean that the false will imprison you. If that's the case, the PC movement is single-handedly responsible for holding us hostage to a trumped-up vocabulary.

In my act, I refer to the fact that cars today, with their multiple air bags, are too safe, contributing to a society of wusses. This obvious satire on our overprotective society leads me to talk about kids today, who I assume have never been in a bagless car: "They probably think the Model T had an air bag, only it wasn't technologically sophisticated, just a midget with a paper sack!"

I'd been performing this routine for years, and it had never occurred to me that it was anything but funny. But one summer, after performing this bit for thousands of men in auditoriums across the country, a midget approached me after the show to say he was offended by the joke. He wasn't hurt by the inference to his shortness but by the use of the word, which he found derogatory. When I asked him what he preferred, he said, "Little people."

You have to understand, folks, that I, myself, am something of a little person, at five-foot-six, and if you called me that, I'd be angry enough to stand eye-to-crotch with you and ask you if you wanted to repeat that to my face . . . or . . . to the top of my head. So it was inconceivable to me that anyone could look at someone as short as me and think I would think less of them. Apparently, one man's honor is another man's insult.

> I, myself, am something of a little person. Though if you called me that, I'd be angry enough to stand eye-to-crotch with you and ask you if you wanted to repeat that to my face . . . or . . . to the top of my head.

But, again, his issue was with the word "midget." I remembered watching a show on physical deformities that stated that "midget" was the term used for people of abnormally short stature but who were evenly proportioned (whereas a dwarf was a person of abnormally short stature whose appendages were not in proportion to the rest of his body). Always in search of obscure knowledge that I can use to give the illusion that I'm smart, I went home and checked my dictionary, which stated that a midget was, indeed, "someone of abnormally small stature, whose limbs are proportionate to their body." In other words, I was right.

Somewhere in the interim between this dictionary's publication and me performing my show, the word "midget" not only went out of vogue, it became slanderous. Through the insidious politically correct movement, liberals have hijacked our language to soothe their oversensitive psyches, whereas the conservative believes calling a midget a "midget" is fine, so long as we're telling the truth.

As a conservative, I find it exhausting to try to keep up with the offensive words of the day, especially since so many words that were changed were much easier to use in their previously offensive incarnation.

Native Americans were simply Indians. I can't speak for the liberal, but as a conservative kid who grew up playing cowboys and Indians, I can say we *all* wanted to be the Indian because, to us, he was a noble and powerful warrior. African Americans were simply black, thus distinguishing them from white (since it's the most obvious descriptive difference), and for some reason, even at the height of the civil rights movement, everyone kind of took their American status for granted and didn't need to define themselves as such. Flight attendants were stewardesses and, God bless 'em, I don't care how many times they change their title, they are still basically beverage servers and pillow fetchers. If this is insulting, maybe a job change rather than a name change will bring the respect they crave.

If a liberal can really call a short person "vertically challenged," and a fat person "metabolically disabled" with a straight face, why isn't a baby "chronologically deficient"? I think conservatives would do everyone in this country a favor if we started redefining existing monikers in our own image in order to demonstrate how manipulative and legally exploitative the lunacy of the liberal actually is. From now on, let's call a man "mammary impaired," thus giving him maternity-leave rights. A college student could be "educationally inexperienced." Were a professor to assert intellectual superiority, the student might be shamed and their self-esteem scarred, which seems like grounds for a lawsuit, don't you think? In an era where feelings are more protected than real initiative or achievement, it appears we need to give everyone who enrolls in college automatic A's so they feel they're getting their money's worth.

> If a liberal can really call a short person "vertically challenged," and a fat person "metabolically disabled" with a straight face, why isn't a baby "chronologically deficient"?

Of course, the list of possible reinventions is endless, and, as a conservative, I have learned well from the liberal to simply identify and demonize my "enemies." Feminists, in the new conservative lexicon, would become "extreme estrogenists." I'd send the fanatical antimale sexists to an island populated only by their kind and see how long they'd survive without someone to move their furniture and change their oil.

And then there's the liberal himself. Democrats would no doubt try to get into the act by simply redefining their "morally deficient" status and renaming themselves "relativistic Republicans," thus having access to both parties' voting constituencies.

Perhaps those Dems aren't so dumb after all.

How Bumper Stickers Can Teach You Religion and Science

I learned to drive in Southern California, where everyone—and I mean *everyone*—proudly displays bumper stickers on their cars. Talk about putting a mustache on the *Mona Lisa*! Maybe I'm crazy, but if you have a hundred-thousand-dollar car . . . I don't care if your kids are on the honor roll, get rid of the bumper sticker! Hopefully, they'll grow up to be smart enough not to stick adhesive on the bumper of a Ferrari!

Now, to be fair, I should also note that I see a lot of my Christian brethren slappin' stickers on their cars. Of course, theirs always have some deep theological meaning. My favorite is GOD IS MY COPILOT. I remember the first time I saw this one; I sped up to see who was driving! I want to know: How good a person do you have to be to get GOD to ride "shotgun"?

I think a good rule of thumb is, if God's in your car . . . LET HIM DRIVE! Why not? He never gets in a wreck and can talk himself out of tickets. He can even knock the radar gun digits back a couple spaces if he needs to. The whole concept of God as the copilot implies that he can't drive better than you. (God: "You take the wheel, I'm not familiar with this area.") Plus, the last thing anyone needs is God as a backseat driver. (God: "That man's swerving!" Me: "Where? I don't see . . ." God: "Three minutes from now!")

> I think a good rule of thumb is, if God's in your car . . . LET HIM DRIVE!

Bumper stickers also tell us a little about the beliefs of our fellow drivers. Have you ever noticed that the quantity of anti-Bush, environmental worship/abortion/leftist stickers someone puts on his bumper is usually in direct proportion to how crappy the cars are? It's as if these people are saying, "Ignore my rundown, beat-up car but look at my profound slogans and follow in my footsteps!" Anyone who believes they're saving the environment while driving a '78 Gremlin needs to get back to the commune immediately for some indoctrination in common sense.

> The quantity of anti-Bush, environmental worship/abortion/leftist stickers someone puts on his car is usually in direct proportion to how crappy the car is.

Then there are the middle/upper-middle-class drivers. They go for the minimalist approach with only one sticker that represents either the sport their child plays, the pyramid scheme they belong to, or their religious persuasion.

Enter the fish. The fish was a secret symbol that started in Roman times so Christians could identify each other without the inconvenience of being eaten by animals. (In Roman times, Christians were thrown to the lions for their beliefs, a custom that eventually died out until recently. In America today, the liberal media has found it fashionable to mock, ridicule, and demean Christians through television and motion pictures. Anytime an intolerant, evil, hypocritical jerk is needed in the script, the liberals say, "Make 'em a Christian. Serves them right for thinking up this 'morals' ploy before we did.")

Christians aren't the only ones championing a religious or philosophical idea that will fit on a bumper. Evolutionists, having no morals (since they don't evolve), mocked the Christian fish symbol by adding feet and spelling "Darwin" inside the fish's body. Gee, for a bunch of intellectuals, you would think one of them might have been creative enough to come up with a sign of their own! Maybe an amoeba riding on a lightning bolt, perched on a cloud of gas?

And why stop at the Christians? Jews believe humanity was created by God, so why aren't the atheists (who believe that humans are an accident of time and molecules in motion) putting fins on the Star of David? Come to think of it, Muslims believe in creation, too. There must be something funny you can add to the crescent moon, to indicate that humans really evolved from dust!

Scientists apparently only feel comfortable ridiculing the majority. They also seem to be ignorant of history when it comes to the relationship between science and faith. They love,

Why stop at the Christians? Why aren't the atheists putting fins on the Star of David?

for example, to cite the idea that Copernicus was considered a heretic for his heliostatic theory that proved the earth revolved around the sun. (And since I'm not that smart, I had to look up "heliostatic theory," and so would anyone who didn't get beat up in school a lot.) But while it appears that Catholics at the time took issue with Copernicus's ideas, it was a Lutheran prince who subsidized the publication of his work, a Lutheran theologian who arranged for the printing, and a Lutheran mathematician who supervised it. So not all of the church disagreed with good old Copernicus, as the atheist scientist revisionists would want you to believe.

How about Isaac Newton? Some consider him the greatest scientist who ever lived. He was a Christian. An atheist would try to turn him into a *deist* but that's a little rough when he wrote things like, "God governs the world invisibly, and he has commanded us to worship him, and no other God . . . He has revived Jesus Christ our redeemer, who has gone into the heavens to receive and prepare a place for us." Blah, blah, blah. James Simpson was a Christian who invented chloroform, obviously to be used on liberals as often as possible. Joseph Lister used antiseptics in operations and gave us the name of that ever-so-difficult-to-gargle product, Listerine. Louis Pasteur was a WASP as well. The list goes on and on.

James Simpson was a Christian who invented chloroform, obviously to be used on liberals as often as possible.

The greatest scientific minds of our time, quite literally those who created modern science as we know it, were Christians who believed that they were observing the handiwork of God. For today's scientists to ridicule what these men believed, and do so in the name of science, is puzzling to say the least. Worse yet is that the liberal refuses to let the same God that inspired Newton into our children's classrooms. Instead, let's just keep teaching our kids that they are an accident, are cousins to apes, and that suing is the quickest way to make a buck.

Speaking of evolution, have we touched on that yet?

☆ 27 ☆

Why Speak English Anyhow?

I refuse to play the "Oh, aren't we sooo pluralistic?" game that goes so far as to not even let me use the word "large" when ordering coffee at Starbucks.

Starbucks is an American company started in Seattle. Why does it pretend it's Italian? When you try to order a simple cup of coffee, the fun begins. Medium is a *grande*. *Grande* means "large" in Spanish, by the way. Which only confuses the matter. Because at Starbucks, *grande* is not large (it's medium), and they aren't trying to be Spanish, but Italian.

What does this have to do with being liberal or conservative? The liberal mind, in its warped state, has convinced much of America that if you speak two words of Italian (even if they are *gran-day lah-tay*), you're multicultural, and that's certainly better than just being American. Why should I feel guilty if I want to speak English at an American establishment of business?

Even Mexico has taken a cue from the doctrine of American liberal minds: When something doesn't go your way, make

The liberal mind has convinced much of America that if you speak two words of Italian, that's better than just being American.

somebody else responsible. Mexico is full of corrupt politicians, local government officials, and lawmakers. They aren't going to change anytime soon, nor do they know or care how to make things better for their impoverished countrymen.

Solution? As I see it, they have two choices: (1) clean up the system by demanding accountability and creating opportunities at home or (2) allow their people to escape illegally across the border into the United States, where you can count on the liberals to embrace them with open arms, huddle them close to their breasts like lost little children, and watch them accuse the conservatives, once again, of their heartlessness. Since we are, of course, dealing with fellow human beings who only want to make a better world for their children by teaching them the honorable character trait of sneaking into a country illegally, then demanding that they have some form of constitutional rights.

Thanks to the liberal mind-set, which insists that *grande* means medium, the poor Mexicans (who only aspire to a better life) feel they have a shot at swimming across the Rio Grande, since it's only a medium river, not a large one . . .

So, medium is *grande* and large is . . . I don't remember. *Venti? Venti*, derived from the Latin word "vent," which is meant to be used in sentences like "I went to Starbucks to order a large coffee and had to VENT my anger at the fact that the medium was *grande,* and when I ordered it I only then realized it was not as *grande* as the *venti,* which I couldn't have known because for some strange reason I never thought it necessary to speak Italian in America IN ORDER TO ORDER A STINKIN' CUP OF COFFEE!!"

Just in case you think I am taking all of this too seriously, I should reveal that Starbucks contributes a lot of money to Democratic causes, so I rest my case. But let me also remind you that they call a small a TALL! See, folks, I'm so backward and out of touch that I can actually remember a time when "tall" meant something was . . . (give me a second to recall those archaic bygone days) . . . NOT SMALL! And even if I protest this exotic name game, I can't win. The baristas (as they call their counter help) have been taught to speak only in the original Starbucks language, and by gosh they aren't going to budge. When you order in English, they will actually translate your order into their terminology as though if they accepted "medium" as a legitimate order without correcting your ignorance, somehow you beat them. Or maybe the guy who is actually making the drink wouldn't follow? To me, it also demonstrates the loss of common courtesy prevalent in the new liberal America that states, "I'll help you up to the point that it inconveniences me, then you can just stick it in your ear."

> The loss of common courtesy prevalent in the new liberal America states, "I'll help you up to the point that it inconveniences me, then you can just stick it in your ear."

It's the same kind of strange phenomenon that takes place in movie theaters when you order a beverage they don't stock, and instead of simply telling you that, they repeat your order back to you with the product they DO carry in its place. So, you go to the concession counter and the dialogue goes something like this:

Beverage Boy: "Can I help you?"
Me: "Yeah, I'd like a Coke."
BB: "Pepsi?"
Me: "No, a Coke."
BB: "Pepsi OK?"
Me: "Um, no, actually. I'll take a 7UP instead."
BB: "How's Sprite?"
Me (getting visibly annoyed): "I'll just have a Dr Pepper."
BB: "We have Mr. Pibb."

Mr. Pibb. Who has Mr. Pibb but not Coke?

I want a language where you can interpret the words to mean anything you want so as to get your way. In my version, it would sound something like this:

BB: "That'll be five bucks."
Me: "Uhh, here's thirty-five cents, thanks."
    And, by the way, I'm leaving you a two-cent tip . . .
    Pretty "grande" of me, don't you think?

☆ 28 ☆

The Liberal Approach to Future Compost

I would think environmentalists would be a little disappointed with Starbucks' ecology record because of their paper cups. The truth is, anything *used* should be a no-no to the ultra-eco-fanatic. A truly committed eco-freak should be expected to drink only coffee that has been poured directly into his cupped hands. Not only is this good for the environment, but his screams would be a poignant reminder to the rest of us how serious his commitment is to all living things—things, he would reason, that are no different from us—unless of course you consider having a body, a conscience, a soul, and the ability to reason somehow "different," but of course that just makes me closed-minded.

Back when I was growing up, paper coffee cups came equipped with cardboard handles that you pulled out in order to not burn your fingers. Nowadays, they double-stack the cups or place a cardboard sleeve around the cups, but fear not, eco-freako, it's made out of recycled paper! In other words, they

went to the dump, pulled out some paper, and cleaned and re-
stored it in order to provide you with twice as much trash! They
couldn't just stick with the cardboard handles that served us well
for thirty years?

All in the name of saving Mother Earth. Good thing we re-
duced those aerosol spray emissions in order to make the air
cleaner for those people traveling to their recycled-paper plant,
where they pollute the air with their eco-friendly brand of
stench. Of course, when an environmentalist pollutes, it's on the
way to a protest, so it doesn't count. If we could bottle their arrogance, we'd make a fortune. Plus, it would give them another
company to protest.

> When an environmentalist pollutes, it's on the
> way to a protest, so it doesn't count.

Somewhere along the line, liberals created the idea that conservatives don't care about the environment, and always associate us with uncaring corporations that pollute indiscriminately.
This theme of "the corporation is always bad" rings hollow
again and again, though, since recycling is big business—and,
by the way, comes in the form of a corporation. The fact that
the liberal-minded are building bigger companies to fix the
problems created by what they'd call, uh, big companies makes
one wonder if they are unfamiliar with the word "irony" (or
maybe they just have a different, less offensive word for it).

The ultimate fun house of illogical liberal eco-ideology is
that for every "bad" company, they create a "good" one to rem-

edy it. For every nature preserve they want to remain unspoiled, they set up base camps, filled with humans who are flying in food (they need to eat), using water (they need to shower), and creating human waste, but, hey, they're there to keep it clean. For every national natural treasure, there is an eco-freak arriving in some kind of gas-powered vehicle to appreciate it. And every eco-blogger waxing philosophic about not disrupting the environment is writing from a home with a refrigerator, microwavable food, and a couple cars parked in their air-conditioned garage.

> For every national natural treasure, there is an eco-freak arriving in some kind of gas-powered vehicle to appreciate it.

Until the serious eco-people live naked, in caves, eating whatever grows on trees and in the ground naturally, using their waste to fertilize crops for the rest of us, maybe they could all do us a favor: Relax, get over themselves, and enjoy a steaming hot handful of coffee. We could use the laugh.

☆ 29 ☆

I Want to Be Old

One of the things all kids should be required to do is to visit an old folks' home on a regular basis so they can learn to appreciate the wisdom of those who have lived for a long time. We are diminishing and disrespecting our old people by shutting them up in homes where all their wisdom and life experience is wasted.

Probably one of the first things this old person would say that would blow a kid's mind is that we used to bring our elderly relatives into our homes to live *with us*. Believe it or not, they'd say, there was once a time when family members were *revered* and taken care of, not shipped off to homes to be tended to by strangers. Elderly weren't considered inconvenient back then, they were actually treasured. But since our liberal-minded society has trained us all to think that what we desire trumps all other responsibilities and obligations, families now send their parents and grandparents to live in a place where the main requirement is that it's not attached to ours. That way we can feel free of guilt and obligation to care for those who gave us life and nurtured us to adulthood, and spend our time on more important concerns, like who's going to win *American Idol*.

> By sending our parents and grandparents away, we can feel free of guilt and obligation, and spend our time on more important concerns, like who's going to win *American Idol*.

Old age frightens the liberal because it exposes a truth long known by the conservative: Life isn't perfect, and it isn't pain-free. It seems most liberals believe that since old age is a time where pain is very much a regular part of daily life, and this reality can't be fixed, it must be removed from our sight. The liberal "reasons" (and I use that term generously): If you have reached a point in your life cycle where you are really more burdensome than beneficial, perhaps we should help you enhance your dignity with the ever-honorable option of doctor-assisted suicide. The alternative is that we could, as a culture, value you to such an extent that we will let God decide when your term is over and do everything in our power to comfort you and embrace your life, hoping to learn all we can to pass on to our children.

The first thing we must do is teach our kids to respect their elders, especially considering the goal of all human beings is to live as long as possible, which, if accomplished, inevitably results in getting old. Young people always look at old people like they're freaks, like they STARTED that way, with double chins and gray hair and bad vision. Like God let them choose one option or the other: "So, do you want to be young and nimble or old and feeble?"

As a Christian, I don't fear getting old because I don't fear death. I, for one, *want* to be old. Old is good because you have acquired wisdom and life experience, not to mention loads of discounts at movies and Denny's. I love the idea of being old because with age comes perspective. When you're old you can finally differentiate between what actually matters in life and what doesn't, since you're asleep half the time anyway.

> Old is good because you have acquired wisdom and life experience, not to mention loads of discounts at movies and Denny's.

I have an eighty-seven-year-old grandma, and I have seen firsthand the freedom that comes with getting old. When you're over eighty, you don't CARE about being popular anymore, you don't CARE about being rich anymore, you don't CARE about clothes that MATCH anymore. I can wrap my grandma up in aluminum foil, and she couldn't care less, she's out the door! The neighbors are used to it by now: "Oh look, there's Jesse in her space suit again!"

The other great thing about old people that we could all learn from in this country? They can take a joke! I love my grandma, but tell me, where does she find her perfume? And is it SUPPOSED to sear the iris? Is that what she's shooting for, 'cause on Grandma, it's not a fragrance, it's a force field! My grandma buys her perfume by the jug. Usually in a floral scent, the only criteria for which is smelling like a flower that doesn't exist in nature (and if it did, it would likely eat the bees). Forget about dabbing it behind the ears, she bathes in it! It's like a homing device for old people, so in case she wanders away, you can find her. "Where's Grandma?" "I don't know (*sniiiifff*). Wait, she's over there in the cupboard with the Tupperware again!"

I'm telling you, folks, I want to be old. I want to sit around as an old man in my favorite chair with my children and grandchildren sitting at my knee waiting for some nugget of wisdom right before my nap . . . I want to drive in the biggest car I can find and stay in the fast lane of the freeway going twelve miles per hour with my turn signal on for no apparent reason whatsoever, while younger people pass me, flipping me off. I just want to sit there, hunched and secure, saying, "I am ninety years old, I fought in the war and paid my taxes, I deserve this lane and I'm not moving . . ."

I want to wear underpants that give me the option of not having to find a restroom when I need one. At the bottom of the ninth with the bases loaded and two outs, after having five big cups of Coke, I want to be the only person at the baseball game who can lean back, relax, and just let it go. I WANT TO BE OLD! Now, if the liberals will just let me get there without cutting me off and putting me to sleep, I know the world will be a better place.

☆ 30 ☆

How Smoking Epitomizes Capitalism

Before anyone knew cigarettes were bad for us, the tobacco industry was working overtime trying to find a way to make inhaled smoke sound appetizing. This, to me, demonstrates the conservative ideal of the free market at work. A company's ability to actually sell you something that tastes terrible and makes you hack like a ninety-five-year-old when you first try it—something that you actually have to go out of your way to get used to in order to talk yourself into spending money on it—is about as good an example of individual freedom as one is likely to find.

A company's ability to actually sell you something that tastes terrible and makes you hack like a ninety-five-year-old when you first try it is about as good an example of individual freedom as one is likely to find.

I think the fact that some people choose to smoke is more an indictment of their lack of rational decision-making than the fact that this product is available for the bargain-basement price of, what, almost ten bucks a pack? We all have free will, and, thanks to the liberal (or so he would think), we also have free choice in this country. (Isn't choice what liberals are always fighting for?) It's fascinating that the same people who believe it's imperative for Americans to have the right to find a physician who is willing to blaspheme his Hippocratic oath by helping someone kill himself is unable to let a smoker choose to kill himself (albeit, much more slowly). Where, exactly, does the self-righteous liberal draw the line between the absolutes of bad and good? They say smoking is bad for us and bad for those exposed to it. But physician-assisted suicide, in the liberal's humanistic philosophy, is somehow *good* for you and surely bears no negative effect on the loved ones left behind.

Some smokers blame Indians (that's "Native Americans" to liberals) for inventing cigarettes. Well, yes, Indians grew tobacco, and, yes, they smoked it, but it was in the form of a peace pipe, reserved to celebrate such occasions as "If you don't massacre my family, we won't scalp yours!" But smokers always blame someone other than themselves for their addiction. You hear them standing outside the office in the smoking area saying, "It's not my fault—I started when I was a kid, and now I can't stop." Yeah, well, you also soiled yourself as a kid, and you know what, YOU GOT OVER IT!

In the context of these conversations, the word "can't" usually translates to "I don't want to." The true statement is either "I don't WANT to stop" or, even more important, "It's really HARD to stop!" This is where the rubber meets the road be-

You hear smokers say, "It's not my fault, I started when I was a kid, and now I can't stop." Yeah, well, you also soiled yourself as a kid, and you got over that!

cause, for the spineless, the fact that something is going to take work or might be unpleasant makes it unfair. In the past, people who were overweight kept an eye on their calorie intake. Now, they get their stomachs stapled. Maybe the solution for smokers who are having difficulty quitting is to have their lips sewn shut? Not only would you stop smoking, you would lose weight at the same time! (That's it, I'm calling a patent attorney.)

For the record, I don't smoke and don't advocate it. The truth is, smoking is weird. Because inhaling smoke into your lungs is not a natural thing to do. Actually, it's something you are usually taught to *avoid*, kinda like keeping your mouth closed while swimming. Back in the early days of man, well before billboards, smoke usually came in the form of a campfire. I find it difficult to visualize some guy sitting around a campfire, suddenly sucking in a lungful and, after recovering from the coughing fit and gasping for air, thinking, Hmmm, how could I package that? (Nevertheless, the fact that he did is once again a tribute to the ingenuity of the American capitalist.) That's why calling a cigarette "smooth" never made sense to me. Who ever came out of a burning building, and, when asked what it was like, answered, "It was smooth. Yeah, I'm going back in there, that was refreshing!"

Indians may have invented smoking, but you sure never saw

one smoking a cigarette in a cowboy movie. That's because even these so-called savages were smart enough to discern that cigarettes are nothing but leaves and paper on fire! If the Indians really did invent smoking, then I say it was a practical joke on the white man. Kind of the whoopee cushion of the Cherokee. Here we were, the white man, taking their land—smoking was their parting gift to us. It must have been hysterical recounting the scenes of "How stupid is the white man?" in the teepee at night:

Chief Running Bear: "Hey cowboy, suck this into your lungs, heep big medicine, and real smooth." (laughter) "He did it! What an idiot!"

Itching Powder: "Running Bear, you're one funny guy. Let's see if he'll fall for another one. Hey, cowboy, if you lick the red hot end . . . uh . . . all your wishes will come true!!" (more laughter)

Running Bear: "Oh, Itching Powder, you're the best!"

Yes, my friends, smoking is bad for you; it stinks and it causes cancer. But dang it, let me make the decision to smoke or not to smoke on my own. Obesity will also kill a lot of Americans, but I don't see any liberals protesting Häagen-Dazs.

That's a truly free society. Not to mention it keeps the seat belt makers in business.

A Reading from the Book of Madge

When I was growing up in Indiana in the late sixties, American families were still in the habit of eating dinner together. Shortly thereafter, somebody (no doubt a liberal more focused on entertainment than on family values) invented TV trays and TV dinners, and, little by little, the family dinner at an actual table was replaced by a Salisbury steak with cherry cobbler, hot out of the oven, served in an aluminum tray, accompanied by Jackie Gleason (drinking a Scotch and smoking a cigarette), single-handedly trying to accomplish President Kennedy's vision by sending his wife, Alice, to the moon.

> Little by little, the family dinner was replaced by a Salisbury steak with cherry cobbler, hot out of the oven, served in an aluminum tray.

It was during these turbulent times that my mom, who was such a throwback that she insisted we still eat at the table, used to serve something called "casserole," which was apparently based on the French word for "Mom didn't shop." Casserole always consisted of a concoction of leftover food from meatloaf to green beans, thrown together in a Pyrex dish and baked for twenty minutes at 350 degrees, which made for an even less tasty dish than the original ingredients were in the first place.

There's a reason why we have food known as leftovers. They are *left over* from the previous meal because nobody liked them the first time around. Combining already rejected food with other ingredients into one colossal meal and expecting your kids to like it makes as much sense as schools offering calculus and history of the accordion classes as an alternative to summer vacation. Had my mother let me eat in front of the TV, I may never have noticed how much I hated this stuff and how it would rank number one in my most-despised-food category until it was finally dethroned in the seventies by quiche.

> Had my mother let me eat in front of the TV, I may never have noticed how much I hated casserole and how it would rank number one in my most-despised-food category until it was dethroned in the seventies by quiche.

The biggest problem with a casserole is that no one ever craves one. No family member, be they adult or child, ever works hard all day, whether at work or at school, longing for a casserole. It just doesn't happen. Even in Dickens's novels, where the kids spend their days being beaten and forced to do hard labor, they at least had the comfort of knowing they'd get a bowl of gruel, since casserole would have been considered cruel.

Another clue that the casserole concoction is going to suck is when it's topped with chow mein noodles, of which there seemed to be a surplus in the seventies, since this is apparently what they used to stuff the ever-popular beanbag chair. When you have a concoction that actually uses chow mein noodles to enhance its flavor, you've got a problem. Kinda like using bologna to spice up a dish. I think my mom instinctively knew that we didn't like casserole, which is why she tried to give it a fancy name to trick us into thinking we were eating something exotic.

"Goulash" casserole was a favorite attempt at culinary decep-tion ("grab-bag casserole" would have been more accurate). Her so-called goulash was a horrific blend of undefined meat prod-uct (smashed) with noodles and some kind of rubber, barf-looking cheese. I would try to reason with her in my most theatrical childlike way ("I can't eat the smashed-up food, Mother, *I just can't*"), and she would retort, "You eat like a bird."

Of course, I was too young to realize that my parents were conservatives, and despite my childlike "need" to feel empow-ered, they were going to make sure I was a respectful, productive member of society irrespective of what I might consider my rights. There is no talking back in a conservative's home. So my sarcasm wasn't exactly seen as free speech, and my mom did what all good conservative moms did when a kid got a little "lippy," which was to wash my mouth out with soap. Now, as you could easily gather, I am absolutely pro-disciplining children by whatever means necessary (short of physical abuse or selling them), but, please tell me, who decided that putting a cleaning agent in a kid's mouth was a rational mode of discipline? I get that it symbolizes washing the nasty remark out of your mouth. But, if that makes sense, why stop there? Why not use all the cleaning products from under the sink to rebuke bad behavior? You know, different stuff for different sins. If I catch you saying a dirty word, you get soap in the mouth; if I catch you reading a dirty magazine, how about Comet in the eyes? At least it would be consistent! If soap is that powerful at washing away our sins, it should have been mentioned in the Bible. It would come down as some kind of prophetic decree: "And the Lord took the man's withered hand and placed it into the dishwashing liquid, and the man removed his hand quickly for he was sore afraid, and the Lord comforted the man and said, 'Fear not . . . it's Palmolive!'"

Thus ends the reading of Madge, chapter 7, verse 3. So let it be written, so let it be done.

☆ 32 ☆

Let There Be Peas on Earth

If there's one point that liberals and conservatives can agree upon, it's that war sucks. Somehow, liberals have drawn the (wrong) conclusion that conservatives like war and killing—and it seems the liberals will battle us tooth and nail to make their point. (Which I guess proves that liberals will fight wars, but only verbal ones, which are only fought at home so that when they lose they can run home to tell their dad or a federal judge, whoever is handiest.) Though there certainly are patriotic liberals who have fought and died in war, their disturbing tendency is to return from war, tell us about the horrors of it (like somehow we didn't know), and then spend their political lives lambasting America for our imperialistic ways.

Trust me—as a conservative, I wish no one will ever die at the hands of an aggressor again. And I don't claim expertise in the intricacies of diplomacy and international affairs. But common sense will tell you (if you're willing to listen) that we have always had war, and we always will. Liberals try to simplify the concept of war with the naive notion that all we have to do is let everyone know we don't want to fight, and then our enemies will just throw down their weapons and leave us alone. Every hard issue is oversimplified by the liberal, and yet war is not an easy rationalization no matter what because it's accompanied by death, and nobody wants that.

> Liberals try to simplify the concept of war: All we have to do is let everyone know we don't want to fight, and then our enemies will just throw down their weapons and leave us alone.

In the sixties, liberals (or "hippies," as they were called then) looked to songs to bring meaning to their lives. Well, songs and pot and free sex, dropping acid and dropping out, but how else could you convince yourself that a Nehru jacket looked cool? This delusion that if you sang out against war it somehow made a difference simply underscores the fact that those in the entertainment industry take themselves *way* too seriously when it comes to their impact on society. Very rarely in our history have songs actually caused us to physically *do* something. The only one that comes to mind right off the bat is the Hokey-Pokey, which tells you where to place your body parts, but, hey, *that's* what it's all about. During the Vietnam era, songs like John Lennon's "Give Peace a Chance" were sung like hymns. Actually, there were lots of songs that ministered to this congregation of future liberal senators. "All You Need Is Love" was one, "Put a Little Love in Your Heart," another. Songs that were so inspiring they compelled undergraduates to bomb colleges and riot, all in the name of love (of course). Unfortunately, just because a song sells well and makes us all feel gooey inside doesn't mean it accurately reflects the way things are.

I, too, wish wars could be avoided just by singing. Then we wouldn't need to send soldiers to the front lines, we could just send *American Idol* finalists or Ashlee Simpson, which would certainly make Bin Laden surrender. But then again, this type of hostile intervention is probably outlawed by the Geneva Convention.

> I, too, wish wars could be avoided just by singing. Then we wouldn't need to send soldiers to the front lines, we could just send *American Idol* finalists or Ashlee Simpson.

The main problem with the "songs for surrender" theory was that liberals only sang them to Americans. For some reason they neglected to get 45s of their favorite love tunes to North Vietnam. Just think, if Pol Pot had heard them . . . what, no killing fields? How *do* songs actually change public policy? How do you give peace a chance if you're the only one being peaceful? Why weren't the liberals singing "give peace a chance" when Osama bin Laden recruited people to blow up innocent Americans in this war he chose to start?

Seems to me that prior to this murderous act of terror we *were* giving peace a chance. But we conservatives discovered the true irony of the human experience long ago: The only way peace has a chance is if we are prepared for and willing to go to war! Most conservatives and many liberals supported the invasion of Iraq because of our belief that there were weapons there that our intelligence told us could be sold to terrorists. When we didn't find weapons in Iraq, the liberals who didn't support the war did a jig while singing the "I told you so" song. Granted, I wish we'd found the weapons, but the glee with which these liberals celebrated was one of the most disturbing political displays in America today.

Only conservatives seem to be willing to risk their political equity with American citizens in order to proactively defend our nation irrespective of what most of Europe thinks. Hey, at least when democracy rules in Iraq, it's one less Middle Eastern theocracy, dictatorship, torture chamber, and/or terrorist training ground. Good will come of this—American and other Western lives will be saved by having at least one Middle Eastern country that we can try to deal with diplomatically in the future.

I think what America needs is more people driven by common sense. There was a time when a professional constitutional scholar wasn't needed to interpret the constitution because we just took it at its word. Today, the liberal always finds some kind of deeper meaning in what the Founding Fathers said. For example? For more than a hundred years, the First Amendment meant that when religious things were displayed on public grounds, nobody should take issue with it. Now, suddenly, it's supposed to mean that these types of displays are unconstitutional and not, in fact, what the Founding Fathers had in mind. Like the liberal really knows that for sure. If the Founding Fathers weren't cool with the religious displays and prayers IN SCHOOL that were part of the public landscape during the time they were alive, doesn't it seem logical that they would have expressed this before the twentieth-century liberals took it upon themselves to figure it out? You know, considering they wrote it and all. Why weren't abortions being performed at taxpayers' expense during the Founding Fathers' lives since that was, according to liberal judges' constitutional interpretation, their intention all along? Why weren't the Founding Fathers protesting capital punishment and demanding Social Security entitlement national health care, gay marriage, no-fault divorce, removal of Nativity scenes from parks, banning Christmas songs in school plays, and outlawing crosses on war memorials and state seals? Why didn't the *actual* people who *actually* wrote the *actual* Constitution fight for these rights? Could it be because they never intended for any of them to be an issue? The further we get away from the founders' conservative views of America, the more liberals will try to rewrite our heritage.

> Why weren't the Founding Fathers protesting capital punishment and demanding Social Security entitlement, national health care, gay marriage, no-fault divorce, and removal of Nativity scenes from parks?

I wish I could convince liberals that, when it comes to war, we need their support as a "united" states. We're all in this together, and I know you want this country to survive as badly as I do, if for no other reason than if our country is taken over by Muslim extremists, they're going to curtail your access to porn on cable. Regardless of your false view of the world, we are in a battle for our lives and our children.

Maybe conservatives can sing their own song about liberals, borrowed from my take on an old song about another irrational dreamer who fought imaginary enemies: "This is their quest, to follow that lie, no matter how hopeless, no matter how far, to fight for the Left without question or pause to be willing to march into court, for a heavenly cause, yet I know if they continue to be true to their fairy-tale quest, that their heart will lie bleeding and calm when they're laid to rest. And the world will be deader for this, cause this man scorned and covered with scars STILL strove with his last ounce of ignorance to reach the unreasonable star."

☆ 33 ☆

The Michael Moore Effect on Voting

If there is any one person in this country who single-handedly represents the most overpaid, overvalued member of society, it's the professional actor. Actors are good at one thing: They pretend to be somebody else for a living. In their world it's called acting, in our world it's called schizophrenia. Far too many Americans seem to have a love affair with these stars, but that's only if they're liberal. The fact that we have a marketing machine within the entertainment community that has effectively taught our kids to respect personality over character is one of the reasons America is so divided in the first place.

Just in case it escaped your notice—which would be hard to imagine, unless you live in a tree—Hollywood controls what Americans are allowed to see on their television sets and in movie theaters. So if you are conservative politically, Christian theologically, and an unabashed patriot/cheerleader for America and its tradition, you are a person who is completely ignored as a character on TV. (Except for the occasional cameo appearance as a sexual deviant, psychotic/serial killer, and insensitive hate-monger, but I guess I shouldn't look a gift horse in the mouth.) But why does Hollywood, the CAPITAL of the blue states, not use my people as characters in their shows?

Let's carefully weigh the evidence and use some statistics, as our liberal friends do whenever they want one of their particular social agendas to appear scientific. Since three out of four Americans consider themselves conservative, and, depending on which poll you accept, at least 70 percent of America considers itself Christian, 90 percent believes in God, and by and large most Americans are proud and unapologetic about their love and belief in this country, the reason you never see us represented on TV is painfully obvious . . . there's simply no market for it! Why would any studio exec in his right mind risk his reputation on a show with a character that would connect to more than 100 million people when all his money is tied up investing in the next Michael Moore TV docudrama that proves George W. Bush shirked his National Guard service and, while on leave, actually masterminded the Manson family murders?

> Three out of four Americans consider themselves conservative. At least 70 percent of America is Christian, and 90 percent believes in God. But liberals say there's no market.

So, as you can clearly see, it really comes down to economics and has nothing at all to do with anti-conservative/Christian bigotry.

The liberal mind already believes that the image someone

conveys is more important than who they actually are. Hollywood elite are constantly tweaking the nose of the conservative
Middle American because they find what we believe to be backward and irrelevant. Why else would we have Hollywood cou-
ples living together for years, refusing to marry, essentially
denying that marriage has meaning or value? The problem with
existing fully engulfed in a subculture that is like-minded to
your own beliefs is that you no longer have the capacity to relate
to or respect the audience of America to which you are most indebted for funding your projects.

Show me a sitcom that has even one character who is Christian
and isn't made out to be a close-minded buffoon. Show me one
drama that features a conservative character who isn't made out to
be evil and manipulative. Somehow, this passes muster with the
network heads, who (one would think) would owe it to their
stockholders (since they are all corporately owned) to represent all
of America including, amazingly enough, *this vast, Christian conservative majority.* My people—Middle Americans—watch lots of
TV and deserve to be accurately reflected and respected, like anyone else being portrayed.

In Hollywood today, someone can make a movie specifically
designed to bring down a sitting president who is in the midst
of fighting a war and do so using false facts and completely

In Hollywood today, someone can make a movie
specifically designed to bring down a sitting president using false facts.

manipulated sound bites and film clips, thereby altering the perception of what is actually true. The fact that a film such as this would win top honors at Cannes (which is in France—gee, what are the odds?) in spite of the fact that it is based on blatant propaganda driven by lies and half-truths should make fair-minded Americans seethe.

When the rubber meets the road and the average American ducks into the voting booth, I believe they are not only *not* influenced by a star's endorsement of a candidate, but that endorsement usually backfires in what I call the "Michael Moore effect" . . . the opinions of the Left help bolster theirs. So if you ever find yourself torn between two candidates, here's a surefire strategy: Just see who Michael Moore supports . . . and vote the opposite.

☆ 34 ☆

Crafted With(out) Pride Somewhere Other Than in the US of A

As a people, we've forgotten how hard it was to achieve what we have because we already have it. As Americans, we have all essentially been born to a rich family where, for many, work consists of finding someone to work for them. The work ethic that built this country has gone the way of the public square and the stocks in which they'd lock your head and hands if you were a "less productive member of society." The community would gather round these lazy folks and laugh, ridicule, and throw cabbage at them. The expectation was hard work and personal responsibility, and those who deviated from it were shamed into to changing their ways.

Shame no longer exists in this country, as morality takes work, and work no longer comes in the form of dignity and pride of craftsmanship, because the liberal mind has perpetuated the idea that you *deserve* anything you want as opposed to having been blessed with the opportunity to try to acquire it. This attitude, of course, makes for a huge difference in the type of character (or lack thereof) being instilled in the next generations.

The Declaration of Independence tried to nip this entitlement tendency in the bud by dutifully explaining exactly what one should expect from this country before signing on to join it. For those of you who don't have a Declaration of Independence handy, there's a section that says, "We hold these truths to be self-evident, that all men are created equal, that they are endowed by their creator with certain inalienable rights, that among these are life, liberty, and the PURSUIT of happiness."

It appears that this is the crux of the constitutional misinterpretation that the liberal mind has fostered in our children. The Declaration of Independence guarantees that the government will do everything in its power to protect and defend your life and your liberty so that you can freely go forth and pursue happiness. Happiness is not a given, and pursuit is not a promise, but a word involving some modicum of energy expended. So— just to be sure we're all clear—there is an implication that there is going to be some work involved. And there's the mere suggestion that if you go for it, desire it, but don't find it . . . it's YOUR FAULT! And yet, the liberal always sees happiness as the government's responsibility, not as a God-given right, which is tough to reconcile with the fact that God is becoming illegal in this country. Lost on the liberal is the concept that hard work was the mentality that fostered the creative spirit that allowed America to become a technological and social juggernaut.

It hasn't always been like this. At the beginning of our technological revolution, Americans were just coming to realize how clever we were, and so in order to create an empire (motivator: good old, red-blooded capitalism), we had to make sure our

The liberal sees happiness as the government's responsibility, not as a God-given right, which is tough to reconcile with the fact that God is becoming illegal in this country.

product was of the highest quality. At this time, we hadn't yet figured out the prudent economic upside to using forced Chinese labor, like we do now, so we went ahead with the old-fashioned concept of doing it ourselves and doing it well. The quality of the products we produced was unprecedented; stuff was made to last a lifetime. Making products to last a lifetime was no doubt easier when the average life span in the 1800s ended soon after taking your first job in the local sawmill at the age of nine.

Shoes, which were a great luxury to many, were amazingly rugged and seemed never to wear out. They were important for one's health and safety, created for the purpose of protecting your feet, not for their ability to make one's legs appear longer and shapelier. Nowadays, shoes are still a luxury for some, considering they are one of the costliest clothing items to purchase. And most are not crafted with pride in the US of A!

I bought some sandals the other day at a store specializing in athletic footwear. Calling sandals athletic footwear, by the way, apparently justifies charging a hundred dollars, and by the looks of them, I am quite certain they will last my lifetime as long as my life ends somewhere near the early part of next week. Now, I'm not sure when I crossed the line to the place in my life where I accepted the fact that a hundred dollars for a pair of shoes is reasonable, but I suppose it's because I'm as stupid as everyone else who considers a hundred dollars a fair price for athletic footwear, as long as it has a small cotton patch logo that somehow transforms it from your average, everyday sandal that actually costs $2.50 to make into a high-tech, scientifically tested, pro-athlete–endorsed, average, everyday pair of sandals with a cotton patch logo. Not to mention the ads that promise me that when I put them on, I'll not only be able to dunk a basketball and run a triathlon, but the chicks will dig me, too. Not that it does a married man much good, but for a hundred dollars I could use a little ego stroke.

> The ads promise that in these shoes I'll not only be able to dunk a basketball and run a triathlon, but the chicks will dig me, too.

But my shoe choice isn't the issue. The issue is how and why Nike and Foot Locker can get away with charging a full-shoe price for sandals, which are, at best, one-third of a shoe. And since I'm not paying for shoelaces, because there are no grommets to hold them, or grommets, because there is no top to attach them to, I want to know why I am still charged full-shoe price for one-third shoe value? When we accept less, yet pay more, we're shooting ourselves in the foot or, in this case, the sandal.

I have the same issue with visors. Visors cost the price of a full hat, yet they are missing that one crucial element that makes a hat a hat and makes it worth the price you pay for it . . . the entire TOP! I'm betting two-to-one odds that some liberal genius looked at a baseball cap and said, "Hey, we can charge the same amount for a hat without the top, and take the excess material and sell it to the sandal makers!" Liberals are the champions of penalizing the financially successful (those who've earned it and deserve it because they've worked hard and know how to make more) by taking their money and reallocating it to those who have less, so they can spend it on lottery tickets and restraining orders.

This is one of the reasons you see American history "reinterpreted" by liberals within our public school system. If the truth ever got out how ruthless the Founding Fathers were in what was expected of us, then the liberal orthodoxy would fly out the window. Back in the old days, if you were homeless, you weren't given government housing, you were given an ax! "Hey Jeremiah, see those trees over there? That's your new duplex!"

Anything you want is waiting for you in this great country. But it's not going to fall out of the sky and end up in your hammock next to your margarita and unused hedge clippers.

☆ 35 ☆

"Hate Crime" Is Redundant

"Hate crime." Sounds nasty, doesn't it? Yet, if you really rack your brain, you'll remember a time in history when the word "crime" was bad enough and people who made it their mission not to get along with the rest of us (and did bad things to emphasize it) were called *criminals*. This was way before the liberals took over the social sciences (or, shall I say, science in general) by demanding that science only be considered "legitimate" if it is naturalistic in its philosophy.

According to the liberal, behavior is no longer something criminals have control over or should be held accountable for. Instead, it's the result of something that "happened" to them that was not *their* fault but society's fault for not taking enough time to truly understand them. In the sixties, for example, then attorney general Ramsey Clark actually said that poverty *causes* crime. That kind of pseudo social science, if true, should have been able to be verified by the exorbitant amount of food theft that happened during the Great Depression, when so many were out of work with families to feed, but of course that isn't what happened. What we did end up with was a lot more hobos than we have today, but not more stealing. Americans back then considered it more honorable to catch an empty train car to Palookaville and eat beans out of a can than to steal from their neighbors.

> During the Great Depression, Americans considered it more honorable to catch an empty train to Palookaville and eat beans out of a can than to steal from their neighbors.

The liberal approach to Darwinian social science has made little Pavlovian dogs out of people trying to prove the point that the condition you find yourself in dictates not only how you behave, but also justifies it. If you come from poverty, for example, then stealing makes sense, and why not, when the only thing in life that matters to you *is* you. As Americans, we live in a country that provides welfare, food stamps, soup kitchens, church food banks, and so forth. It is virtually impossible to starve to death in the United States. Sure, it's possible to not have the overabundance that most Americans enjoy compared to the rest of the world, but if you want to eat, there is a way to get food. Liberals always talk of ending poverty but have never done it because they are unable to admit that some people are hungry because of bad choices they've made in their lives, and giving them more money, believe it or not, does not equate to making them responsible.

I am not making a case for throwing the poor out in the street, as my Judeo-Christian ethic demands that I have compassion for them. Where the liberal and conservative constantly differ is here: Sometimes true compassion comes in the form of creating scenarios where freedom from your dilemma is in direct proportion to how hard you work at freeing *yourself*. The point being that no matter the situation in which you find yourself, right and wrong are absolutes, and a crime is still a crime.

The idea of a hate crime, though, seems somehow to defy the scientific logic of not blaming the behavior, but highlighting *gradations* of bad behavior that are more or less offensive. For all of you, like myself, who aren't in Mensa, let me define a hate crime for you: If you kill me, it's bad, but if you kill me because you hate conservatives, then that's really bad!

For all of you not in Mensa, here's the definition of a hate crime: If you kill me, it's bad, but if you kill me because you hate conservatives, then that's really bad.

Then again, since it's the liberal who created the hate crime concept, to them, killing a conservative wouldn't be hate, it would be considered self-defense. Seems the idea of a hate crime is reserved for minorities, so only if you're Hispanic, Asian, Jewish, black, gay, or transsexual/transgendered and someone kills you because of it, then that crime is especially heinous.

In my book (and it's my book, so I can say what I want!), murder is murder, so the term "hate crime" is redundant. Every crime is a hate crime, whether it's motivated by hating someone's differences or hating something they have that you don't. You may hate the fact that we have outlawed hate. Hating the fact that you haven't achieved what you wanted out of life or hating your job, your boss, your spouse, or the fact that society has instituted rules that deny you any and everything you desire is not a good enough reason to commit a crime.

Conservatives believe that people should be held accountable for their actions. Liberals *hate* that.

☆ 36 ☆

I Want to Wear Fur Underwear

I like animals as much as the next guy. I want them protected from abuse and inhumane acts as much as anyone else. They can be cute, playful, and make great companions for humans.

But what is even more important to understanding my position on animals is understanding that only *I,* a human, can take a position based on thoughtful contemplation, and only *I,* as a human, can make these statements. And only *you,* as a human, can read and comprehend them, and agree or disagree for reasons of your own. The reason is quite simple, though the liberal would wince at my directness: *It's because animals are beneath us.* Which is exactly why the conservative works to protect them, because they are innocent, because they are vulnerable, because they can't protect themselves. Yet, conservatives never make the leap from seeing animals as a positive addition in our lives to animals having a right to a college education.

God created animals for humans to utilize for *our* well-being. Not the other way around. We eat them, use their milk, utilize

> Conservatives never make the leap from seeing animals as a positive addition in our lives to animals having a right to a college education.

them in research to create lifesaving drugs, and even use their coats as warmth because that was his plan, for the animals and for us. Since the liberal doesn't believe in our God, it actually makes sense that the liberal wouldn't subscribe to our worldview. And, since the liberal believes that animals are equal to himself (there's a joke there, but I'll stay on point), they don't look at their fur as a sports coat, in the way a conservative might. They cry, "Don't wear fur," but for years you rarely heard, "Don't wear leather," until they got wise to their inconsistency. Leather is DRIED MEAT for crying out loud. Liberals routinely spend five hundred dollars to wear beef jerky with a zipper, but they're firm on fur. Now, THAT is weird.

> Liberals routinely spend five hundred dollars to wear beef jerky with a zipper, but they're firm on fur.

Much of the outrage toward the human use of animals by the animal-rights fanatics comes with the term "inhumane." Liberals should think long and hard about the use of that term. If the concern is that we're treating someone or something *inhumanely,* that assumes that human is the standard. (No one is ever accused of treating an animal in*animally* because that would be less heinous. And ridiculous.) If an animal can be used for food, which is a human necessity, then why can't it be used for clothing, which is also a necessity? Even conservative animal lovers—and there are plenty of us—don't expect all of humanity to become vegetarian and only wear nonanimal fabrics!

What's most interesting about the liberal misperception of elevated animal status is that the more they care about animals, the less it seems they think of humans. Their inability to separate themselves from their lack of logic is hysterical until somebody gets hurt. Eco-terrorists will set ablaze a hundred Humvees, sending poisonous gases and all kinds of pollutants into the air—all in the name of protesting automobile pollution. They'll plant metal spikes in trees to maim or kill lumberjacks who not only harvest the wood for human use, but are often the very people to plant the trees in the first place. The idea of saving nature over humanity means all existing humans must go. Gee, if they kill off all of humanity to save the natural world, then that means *they'd* have to go, too, which would be a drag because then they wouldn't be around to know that they won!

When the "Don't wear fur" campaign began in the early nineties, activists used well-known models to be the face of the cause in their print ads. The ad went something like, "I'd rather wear nothing than wear fur." Now, I don't remember the exact quote because, of course, being a guy, I was too busy looking at the girl to appreciate the tag line. And it doesn't make any sense to me to use a naked chick to try and convince people to take your message seriously and to reverse a behavior (like wearing fur) that's been around for thousands of years, but who am I to complain?

Morality is the only possible reason not to use animal fur, but the morality of the animal-rights fanatic differs drastically from the Judeo-Christian model conservatives use. Remember, the anti-fur people were the ones who called people who wear fur "murderers." When you have reached the point when you've convinced yourself that killing an animal is "murder" but killing an unborn human is "choice," then you, sir, are as dangerous as it gets.

That said, these geniuses have created a way that they believe has rectified this situation by creating an industry that manufactures "pretend" materials that replicate fur and leather, and have christened it "faux." *Faux* fur, *faux* leather, whatever they think is off limits to human consumption can be replicated to *look* like mink without removing it from a real mink. If you ask me, the only publicity a mink ever got was from being a stole!

The only publicity a mink ever got was from being a stole!

I'm all for free enterprise. But again, common sense prevails. If you're making synthetic anything, it comes from the same family as plastics and/or any other "nonnatural" substance, which means you may have more minks, but you also have more pollution and more landfills in which you need to bury the non-biodegradable faux. Unfortunately, faux stuff doesn't translate into faux trash.

Another problem with the liberals' *faux* solution is that, in order for faux to be effective, it has to fool the rest of us into thinking it's real, which basically glamorizes the look and defeats the purpose. If you are going to the trouble to counterfeit the look of the very thing you're fighting against, unless you're wearing a sign on your back that reads IT'S FAUX, you're inadvertently advocating it. And if it's a really good replica, *people think it's real!*

To be effective, it makes sense to use different and unusual materials and to make them so compelling that they become the new rage. We've already run the gamut of cotton and wool blends; maybe it's time to glorify something else. When's the last time you saw a really good-looking suit of armor on a runway? Worn with an attractive pump, of course! We could also get into wearing vegetables, which would have the added benefit of promoting the vegetarian diet that many of the most notorious models espouse. Not that models actually have to be vegetarians when they achieve the same results from an IV drip of Diet Coke and a carton of cigarettes an hour.

Yes, vegetables would seem the most obvious underutilized apparel commodity on the market. Carrots and peas strung together into a beautiful macramé gown symbolizing the connection between human and organic farming. That is, until the vegetable-rights advocates begin to make some headway in the national conscience, then you're in for a fight.

The sad truth is that these loons have already started to promote faux food in the form of tofu "turkey," tofu "bologna," and tofu "ice cream." I didn't even know it was possible to make bologna taste worse than it already does, but I guess they want to reach out to those with a discriminating palate who are best able to appreciate the various subtleties of bland.

But back to fur. The truth is, I could care less that they don't want me to wear fur. What I *do* care about is not being able to wear it *if I choose*. What if one day I *wanted* to wear fur underwear? I want the choice to have fur seat covers, fur rugs, and fur wallpaper. When I go to the store and they ask me if I prefer paper or plastic bags, I want to scream "fur!"

In my opinion, murdering an animal is the equivalent to cannibalizing a turnip—you boiled it, you ate it, and how is that not the same? When the liberal who sees an animal as being as valuable as a person and fights to keep others from utilizing animal products almost as vigorously as they fight for the right to abort humans, we live in a society that has truly lost its moral center.

Thanks to the ACLU, we Americans have the privilege of seeing what a culture looks like when its intellectual elite boasts the reasoning power of children: Either they get their way irrespective of the democratic majority or they're just going to sit there and scream!

While they believe they fight for fairness, the conservative knows it's only *faux* fairness.

☆ 37 ☆

Everybody's a Bigot

I have a revelation for you . . . everyone's a bigot. What you are bigoted ABOUT is the question. Now, in case you don't have your dictionary handy, the definition of "bigot" is a person who is utterly "intolerant of any creed, belief, or opinion that differs from one's own." Through their own shortsightedness, liberals have taught us all to wrongly associate the word "bigot" with something inarguably negative. But, the thoughtful conservative should ask himself, is the word inherently negative, or just the speaker using it?

For example, I am bigoted toward the idea of communism. So were the Founding Fathers, as democracy and communism can't coexist. We all are bigoted toward the opinion of terrorists that all Western ideas and ideals should be destroyed. Not only are we intolerant of it, but we will kill to defend our right to refuse to tolerate it.

Whenever the word "bigot" is used, however, it instantly conjures up ideas of the sixties and the equal rights movement of black Americans. I think they were black back then. No, wait

We all are bigoted toward the opinion of terrorists that all Western ideas and ideals should be
destroyed.

a minute, when I reread the statements and letters by Martin Luther King Jr., I realize the proper reference was "Negro." King specifically referred to his cause as a fight for equality for Negroes. Now, I'm not sure when they became black, but it must have been sometime in the late sixties or seventies when we had black-pride movements and blaxploitation movies like *Shaft,* in which the title character was a strong black man, not a Negro private eye.

There may be some debate as to what African Americans prefer to be called, but there is no debate that one of the most abused people that have ever entered into this great American experiment was the African, who was forcefully taken from his home and brought here to be utilized as a slave. It is a sad stain on the history of our country, and one that even the founding fathers knew wouldn't last if this country's ideals were ever to be manifested completely. I admire black Americans for their incredible fortitude in the midst of unimaginable horrors, and in spite of their unfair plight at the beginning of this country, they have gone on in a few hundred years to reach the ranks of secretary of state, CEO, and world-renowned athlete. Under unprecedented handicaps they have accomplished great things, which, in the end, proves that the American dream is real.

When talking recently to a friend of mine who is of a darker hue, I thought it was interesting how he changed his self-references three times within the course of a conversation. Within twenty minutes, he referred to himself and his heritage as "black," "African American," and even "people of color." What's that about? Have the liberal PC word police so infiltrated our psyches that people are careful not to offend even *themselves?* But he also made a statement that got me thinking about the idea of bigotry in the form of racism. He told me that an African American couldn't be racist. When I questioned him on this point, he said that you cannot be racist unless you belong to the race that is in power.

> Have the liberal PC word police so infiltrated our psyches that people are careful not to offend even *themselves?*

I believe that when we speak of racism, most people assume we are talking about the idea of superiority. The problem with this presupposition is that there appear to be areas in which certain races excel, but, for some reason, we are afraid to talk about it. What is insensitive about the obvious fact that for the most part blacks jump higher than whites when we reach the level of elite athlete? Your challenge is to learn how to either overcome this or find ways to enhance your own gifts in order to achieve the best you can for yourself and your family.

Comedy is a way of helping us to acknowledge our differences and, more important, find humor in them. Richard Pryor made an art form out of the way he compared how white people do things versus blacks, and, in the end, what we found in these "racist" remarks was not a divisive exploration but *common ground*. Whites were able to see how we were seen by blacks, and we laughed at ourselves. Where would black comics be if they were not allowed to make fun of the way whites dance? Who hasn't heard this observation a million times? *AND WHO HASN'T LAUGHED?*

Baryshnikov and Nureyev, Fred Astaire and Bob Fosse prove the "can't dance" assumption wrong. So why is this "racist" statement funny? Because it allows us to laugh at our differences instead of fight about them, which can bring us closer as Americans. The statement that "white folks can't dance" clearly isn't true in all cases, but we find it funny because, from the African American perspective, it simply means white people don't dance like *them!* Not being threatened by statements like these allows us to find humor in those places where we don't really relate, where we are more different than the same, which allows us to be honest with each other, the essential starting point to finding common ground.

So, to put my money where my mouth is, I'm going to admit to my racial inequalities. I can't jump, I can't dance, I can't rap, I can't play jazz, I can't run fast, I can't keep time, and I don't clap on the downbeat. Funny, even with all my handicaps, I don't think any less of myself since I always chose to use my inadequacies to drive me, instead of to destroy me. The only thing that worries me now is why I suddenly have a craving for goulash and polka music.

☆ 38 ☆

I Hate Weather Whiners

One of the best things about being conservative is that you learn to be grateful for what you have instead of obsessing over and complaining about what you don't have. Some people—and you know who you are—are like that. It seems they are only completely happy when they are miserable. And one of their favorite topics, since there's usually a fifty-fifty chance they'll be disappointed, is the weather.

Why do people—who are probably liberal, but we'll leave it at people—seem to think that the weather should line up with their plans and their whims and even get *angry* at the weatherman if he gives them a gloomy report? Maybe because the weatherman has been toying with us for years, just waiting to see how long he could get away with general, completely unhelpful, and dubious forecasts. I love it when he gives a report like, "Today, look for a fifty percent chance of rain." Every one of us, through the years, has heard that exact forecast thousands of times and never once questioned its uselessness. The guy actually said "a fifty percent chance of rain." Is there any other job in the world that lets you be that vague? Now, I'm assuming he went to college and got a degree in meteorology so that he could authoritatively say this: "Hey, guys, it might rain . . . it might not!" I never spent a day in college, yet I am pretty convinced I could wake up every single day for the rest of my life, not even look out the window, and say to my wife, "Hey, babe, it might rain . . . it might not." AND I'D BE RIGHT!

Weathermen—or should I say "weatherpeople"—(no, I'll stick with "weathermen" since liberals would advise me otherwise), are such a nuisance when they could be so much more interesting, and the networks finally realized this, so they've tried to spice things up by finding someone who could make "a cold front coming south from Canada" sound entertaining. Apparently, it worked, because some brainiac came up with the idea of a twenty-four-hour channel devoted to . . . weather. (Does that not sound like something you'd expect to see on a *Saturday Night Live* skit?)

The only thing worse than a weatherMAN is a "weather whiner," which I define as anyone who would rather complain about the weather than move to a place with weather they want. Instead, you hear the same old tired saw, "Oh, it's sooooo cold." Why do people actually think they need to tell the rest of us what the weather feels like? Perhaps they're the *real* weather-MAN, the ones who feel it's their *duty* to interpret the atmosphere and announce to the rest of us what the weather feels like to them. And as a true conservative, grateful for what he has rather than what he doesn't, let me say that no matter how bad you think the weather is where you are, there is always someplace worse. I was in Winnipeg, Canada, once in January. It was seventy below. SevenTY! Yet people LIVE there . . . on purpose! I could understand if it was a place of exile. But Winnipeg in January takes exile to new heights. It's so extreme it's the kind of place you'd be sent to if you'd misbehaved in HELL.

> I was in Winnipeg, Canada, once in January. It was seventy below. It's so extreme it's the kind of place you'd be sent to if you'd misbehaved in HELL.

But people choose to live there with their families. I was there to work, take the money, and RUN so I tried to reason with them, "Hey, it's seventy below . . . something's BRO-KEN!" But all the Canadians were like, "Oh, you should have been here last year, it was really cold!" (That's when I really began to have a fresh respect for the Canadians because they weren't complaining, they were adapting!) I, on the other hand, did my show, got my dough, and got the heck outta there. I personally would not want to live in a place where seventy below is considered . . . nippy. I don't want to live in a place where you go out to get the mail, and then you die! I don't want to live in a place where everybody smokes because nobody WANTS to prolong their life expectancy.

The truth of the matter is, some people will never be satisfied no matter what the weather. Pull them out of the cold and put them somewhere hot, and what do they do? Complain! I have been to Las Vegas many times to do gigs. It's an interesting place to visit especially if you hate saving money. The first time I ever went to Vegas was in the month of July. By the way, anyone thinking of taking a family getaway to Vegas in July? Do yourself a favor and club yourself over the head with a blunt instrument. That one act alone will save you a thousand bucks and heatstroke. Why? Because it's 120 degrees there, and you know what? It should be! It's the desert! There were actually people there who were complaining, "It's sooo hot!" Do these people go swimming and complain, "Oh, the water is so wet!" With that kind of insight into the obvious, I predict they have a 50 percent chance of surviving the day without walking into an open MANhole cover!

The problem is not that it's hot in the desert, the problem is someone built a city there. That's why I choose not to live there. No whining, just discretion, my friends. Big difference.

Why Sex Is God to the Liberal

Thanks to liberal relativists, what has become the absolute epitome in recreation for postmodern American now is unequivocally . . . sex. The very nature of the sexual experience is so powerful and so internally robust that it is used even to sell products that have absolutely nothing to do with sex. Any cursory glance around an auto mechanic's shop is all it takes to confirm this self-evident fact. The superior quality of the latest socket wrench kind of becomes muddled when that same wrench is being held by a bikini-clad female posing in a calendar. *She* may be determined that you use this particular brand of tool, but any guy looking at that calendar who has even noticed that there *was* a tool involved must be a former member of the Vienna Boys' Choir. Talk about wasting your time. If there's a nearly naked girl involved in your ad, forget about anyone remembering your product—it's going to get lost in the shuffle since a guy's libido is easily exploited. 'Course when our liberal society winks and looks the other way, it's essentially making this behavior acceptable. "Boys will be boys" is the name of that marketing game.

That, by the way, is an idiom that has never worked for me because it is so incoherent. There must have been a lot of creativity expended to come up with that little nugget. The highly paid ad agency probably tried out a few other alternatives, things like "Boys will be . . . cheese?" and thought, Hmmm, maybe not, any other suggestions? Who is writing these pearls of American wisdom? They make even Yogi Berra sound like Keats.

"Boys will be . . . cheese?" Who's writing these pearls of American wisdom? They make Yogi Berra sound like Keats.

But once the liberal mind-set decided that a urine-filled jar containing a crucifix was art, pornography somehow assumed an equal place in the ideology that nothing is sacred, *including* the sacred. And yet, whether we like it or not, pornography seems here to stay because it represents big money, which used to be the liberal's main target of injustice until the liberal got a piece of the action and justified it as another wonderful example of what the First Amendment was intended for. I'm sure most of the Founding Fathers envisioned a day when women in handcuffs and leather masks would be marched around by a man in a Little Bo Peep outfit wielding a whip as a way of celebrating exactly what a democracy stood for.

Now, conservatives and liberal mind-sets even see sex differently. The *purpose* of sex from the liberal POV is to have plea-

I'm sure most of the Founding Fathers envisioned a day when women in handcuffs and leather masks would be marched around by a man in a Little Bo Peep outfit wielding a whip.

sure. The problem is, that presupposition is wrong. There are many things our bodies find pleasurable, but the pleasure is a wonderful by-product to the actual purpose of the act. We find pleasure in eating, yet we don't consider the purpose of eating to be able to keep Krispy Kreme Doughnuts in business. No, the purpose of eating is so that you don't die! Some people find pleasure in running, though its purpose is to exercise, catch something, or flee from someone chasing you with a two-by-four. We find pleasure in watching our kids in a preschool play even though the purpose of attending the play is to avoid being brought up in their therapy sessions when they're adults and are lamenting that their parents never showed up to watch their interpretation of a rutabaga in their "Tribute to Funny-Sounding Vegetables" school play extravaganza. The inability of the liberal mind to rank restraint over desire renders them unable to articulate their reasons for their positions beyond, "It feels right." What makes the idea of individual desire defining morality is that it becomes problematic when it begins to become mainstream.

The conservative mind sees sex as . . . take a deep breath . . . holy. It is to be engaged in with full force, uninhibitedly, and with great gusto, but it is so important that the only limit to its indulgence is that it is designed for one man and one woman who have promised it to no one else for the rest of their lives.

Suddenly, under those conditions, sex isn't sex for the sake of sex, but an act of giving love at its most intimate all the while creating the possibility of having a child. Remember, the Judeo-Christian ethic states that we are made in the image of God, and so procreation is our way of being fruitful and multiplying more of God's creation through an act of our own will. It is a celebration of the privilege God entrusted us with and, consequently, it comes with a perimeter and a price, as all privileges do. God considered it *so* important to the order of things as to demand that we love our lover to such an extreme that we promise never to leave them or to seek another. Not quite what the liberal had in mind in his view of a life self-absorbed.

To pretend that the temptation for pure hedonism isn't there would be untrue, but it's a little like making a sled out of a Rembrandt—sure, it's a fun ride down the hill, but in the act, you're destroying a masterpiece. Liberals have taught our children that conservatives are repressed when it comes to sex and don't value it the way they do, yet even Freud considered pretty much every human act motivated by repressed sexuality. But as C. S. Lewis pointed out, repression is subconscious, and there is a difference between repression and *suppression,* which is the conscious control of one's impulses. The liberal has made an art form out of unlimited behavioral choices and then used their judges to claim its constitutionality.

The Judeo-Christian ethic that our forebears tried to subscribe to, admittedly if only in theory, was this: "Either marriage with complete faithfulness to your partner or total abstinence." Again, Lewis's brilliant analysis was summed up by stating this type of disciplined expectation regarding our sexual urges is so "difficult and so contrary to our instinct that either the rule is wrong or our sexual instinct, as it now is, has gone wrong."

I am a conservative Christian, and yet, if given the go-ahead by God for sex anytime, anywhere, with anybody, I would be first in line at the Caligula memorial interactive display. But I suppress for what I consider a noble commitment to my wife, and to provide my daughter with an example of what she should expect from a husband. So, I say to the sexually "liberated" liberal American, where you will cry, "More condoms," me and mine will cry, "More character." Both notions are protected speech, but at least ours comes without the complimentary vial of penicillin.

☆ 40 ☆

What It Means to Be a Christian Freak

Coming to the last chapter always carries with it a hint of melancholy. I mean, I've devoted close to a whole Sunday afternoon putting this book together, and to think that it all comes to an end thirty minutes from now would cause even the strongest man to well up just a bit.

I am a know-nothing Indiana farm boy who was brought up with good, old-fashioned Christian/conservative values. To think that one day those ideas would reveal themselves through the format of comedy at a critical time in my country when millions of my fellow Americans are asking who we (conservative Christians) are still amazes me.

Part of the fun and, I think, responsibility of the comedian is to be a gadfly in his approach to evaluating life and ideas. Just because there is absolute truth out there doesn't mean the purveyors of that truth are doing it right.

I am finally at that place that the liberals would deem appropriate, which is being allowed to make fun of your own. I am an expert on the way Christians think because I am one. I grew up going to church and being part of that community pretty much my whole life. I actually had "church" clothes, which were pretty fancy for an eight-year-old boy and usually came with a dickey. I barely remember what a dickey is, but I think it was some kind of false front representing a turtleneck shirt, which begs the question, Why not just wear a turtleneck shirt?

> I grew up going to church. I actually had church clothes, which usually came with a dickey.

I was "saved" in fourth grade. For those of you who are Christian-illiterate and unfamiliar with the meaning of the phrase "saved" or its companion interchangeable term "born again," it's simply a way to describe that you have been made more keenly aware of just how pathetic you are. This idea would never fly among liberals, of course, as their insistence on self-esteem has taught their kids the modern art of defining everything you do as somehow either good, well intentioned, or, when all else fails, misunderstood. To become "born again," in Christian terms, refers to Jesus' proclamation in the Gospel according to John (chapter 3, verse 3) when Jesus said, "Verily, verily, I say unto thee, except a man be born again, he cannot see the kingdom of God." Which is basically Jesus' way of saying, if you want a shot at heaven, you're going to have to start over and let me handle it from here.

So you can certainly see my dilemma in becoming a Christian in fourth grade without the life experience to truly analyze where

To become "born again" is basically Jesus' way of saying, if you want a shot at heaven, you're going to have to start over and let me handle it from here.

I was coming from as a human being. That left out a lot of the soul-searching opportunities that usually accompany those who make spiritual decisions as adults. What it meant for me was that I knew God at a young age, but it made for a real boring testimony. "Testimony" is another Christian term, the equivalent of an AA meeting where like-minded people try to outdo each other in proving that their lives have been tougher than everyone else's. The problem was, my testimony wasn't nearly as cool as the adults who'd had a lot more time to sin than I did. And as a "good" Christian boy, I, too, wanted to impress my fellow Christians with a former life of debauchery, but I had very little to draw from. Oh, how I longed to have a dramatic testimony like, "Yes, I used to be addicted to heroin, and the Lord freed me!" Instead, I would sit in my pew, frustrated that someone else could say, "I was a prostitute and I have come through this ordeal to find a better life." Being a stupid kid, I would think, I COULD HAVE DONE THAT!! Only I didn't even know what a prostitute was . . . Mine ended up being something pathetic like, "Yes, I used to have difficulty with . . . umm . . . long division . . . and the Lord freed me . . . from my . . . uh . . . mathematical shackles." And so began the long arduous journey of self-exploration and the philosophical pursuits that led me to finally and fully embrace the idea of becoming a committed theist.

> Oh, how I longed to have a dramatic testimony like, "Yes, I used to be addicted to heroin, and the Lord freed me!"

I want to acknowledge that the idea of God is not an easy one to deal with in a pool of people with so many differences of opinion. Nor do I pretend that believing in God is always simple. All belief systems that deal with elements of faith can be considered suspect by those who don't subscribe to the same dogma.

Now you know why I'm a conservative. My comedy is given back to my like-minded brethren simply because they deserve a good laugh, too. I realize that since I don't cuss, I'm not nearly as sophisticated and relevant as the liberal comic, but that's the cross I've chosen to bear. I ask nothing from the liberal-minded rulers of the media, for I expect nothing in return. Sure, I'd like the chance at a sitcom like every other comic in the country, but convincing liberal network programmers that conservative Christian in-your-face comedy is "hot" is as likely as using a wishing well to win the lottery. But I'm not giving up. I'm an American, by golly.

> I realize that since I don't cuss, I'm not nearly as sophisticated as the liberal comic, but that's the cross I've chosen to bear.

I *have* found comedy to be a wonderful equalizer, though, that actually helps Americans who hail from different points of view come together, if for a moment, and share the commonness of the human condition. I have loved the opportunities that God has given me to perform for and meet some amazing people, some conservative, some not. But I have found my fans, and I am ever grateful for their passion and support for what I do and how I do it.

My mission was and is to give Americans who think like me a place at the table of entertainment and ideas. I love my God, my family, my country, and, yes, even liberals. I know there is hope for commonality as I have watched the former full-blown liberal Ron Silver articulately and fairly acknowledge the Right policies of President Bush in trying to change the landscape of the Middle East! Even Jane Fonda recently became a Christian, so there is hope! Two down and 50 million to go.

This country is the greatest there has ever been.

Thanks for reading; hope you had fun.

God bless America.

☆ ABOUT THE AUTHOR ☆

BRAD STINE is a conservative comedian, one of three found in the Western Hemisphere. A native of Indiana, he spent several years in L.A., honing his stand-up routine (in addition to his fire-eating, sword-swallowing, magic act), appearing on MTV's *Half-Hour Comedy Hour,* Showtime's *Comedy Club Network,* and A&E's *Caroline's Comedy Hour, Evening at the Improv,* and *Comedy on the Road.* Eventually, he decided (with a few signs from the Big Guy) to focus his act on the two things that mattered most in his life: his contention that America is the greatest country on the planet (that is, before the liberals went and ruined it) and his belief in Jesus Christ.

Stine didn't set out to break convention, but he soon became known as America's favorite conservative comedian, a proud patriot who enjoys shattering preconceptions (both red and blue). Beginning in 2003, he has appeared as the featured performer on the Promise Keepers' 18-city tour and also began touring comedy clubs, college campuses, youth camps, churches, festivals, and fairs to promote his three DVDs, *Put a Helmet On!* (2003), *A Conservative Unleashed* (2004), and *Tolerate This!* (2005)—his first project as a Warner Bros. recording artist. In addition to being the focus of a feature in the *New Yorker,* he has appeared on NPR's *Fresh Air* and *On Point,* and on the *NBC Nightly News, Hannity & Colmes, Paula Zahn,* CNN, the *700 Club,* and in *Newsweek, USA Today,* the *New York Times,* the *Christian Science Monitor,* and the *Chicago Tribune.*

Brad lives in Nashville, Tennessee, with his wife and kids.